Discovering
Cardiff's Past

DENNIS MORGAN

1995
D. BROWN & SONS LTD.
COWBRIDGE

ISBN 1 872808 38 7

Printed in Wales by:
D. Brown & Sons Ltd., Cowbridge & Bridgend, Glamorgan

CONTENTS

ACKNOWLEDGEMENTS

Many people have helped me in the writing of this book. I would like to thank Mr. Bob Morris and his colleagues in the Administrative and Legal Services Department at the City Hall for answering many queries relevant to my research. Similarly, Mr. Mathew Williams, Keeper of Collections at Cardiff Castle, provided me with photographs and information relating to the castle and the Bute family. I have acknowledged the sources of my illustrations elsewhere but I should like to mention the assistance I have received from the following sources: Mr. Stewart Williams, publisher of the *Cardiff Yesterday* series; Mr. Bryn Owen of the Welch Regiment Museum; Mr. Jeremy Glenn of the South Wales Police Museum; and Mrs. Diane Walker. I am also grateful to Jarrold Publishing, whose map in the *Cardiff City Guide* acted as a basis for my own.

It would be impossible to compile a book of this type without first class library facilities. I am indebted to Mr. Bryn Jones for the assistance he gave me in using and selecting material from the splendid resources in the Local Studies Department of the Cardiff Central Library. I also appreciate the co-operation I received from former colleagues in the library at the Cardiff Institute of Higher Education.

In compiling the book, Mr. Dennis Pope processed my photographs in his usual professional manner and, at D. Brown and Sons, Mr. Bob Whitaker gave me the benefit of his considerable experience in the printing industry. Mr. Geoff Dart, who has a profound knowledge of Cardiff and its history, was kind enough to consider the accuracy of my text but, if any flaws remain, they are my responsibility alone.

My family has again been supportive in their encouragement and practical help. Ian has produced many of the photographs, in addition to fighting my battles against the mysteries of computer technology. My wife, Val, has checked my work and made many useful suggestions. She is my inspiration and it is appropriate that I dedicate this book to her.

ILLUSTRATIONS

THE COAT-OF-ARMS OF CARDIFF

The various components that make up Cardiff's elaborate coat-of-arms have evolved through the centuries as a combination of history and legend. At the centre-piece of the banner, the fiery Red Dragon of Wales plants a standard firmly into a green hillock which may represent the mound of the keep in Cardiff Castle. As the flag is thrust into the soil, so the leek, which is of course the national emblem of Wales, springs forth bearing its purple blossom. Of particular interest on the badge are the 3 chevronels that have a connection both with the Welsh and the Norman history of Cardiff.

According to tradition the chevronels of silver upon a red background were the insignia of Iestyn ap Gwrgant, the last Welsh king of Morgannwg. He was an ancestor of the Aberpergwm family from Glynneath and, at the rear of the Mid-Glamorgan County Hall in North Road, a pillar from the driveway of Aberpergwm Hall displays a coat-of-arms on which the chevronels are prominent.

Aberpergwm Arms
at the rear of the
Mid-Glamorgan
County Hall.
(Ian Morgan).

Despite the presence of the dragon, it was not Iestyn who was responsible for the mound on the Castle Green. This was the work of Robert Fitzhamon, a Norman knight who conquered Morgannwg towards the end of the eleventh century and built a motte and bailey castle in the north-west corner of the old Roman fort. Iestyn's fate, upon losing the decisive battle against the Normans at a site known as the "Bloody Brook" in Rhiwbina, is unknown but one legend claims that he became a monk at Keynsham Abbey near Bristol, while another maintains that he was slain and buried locally under a mound known as the "Twmpath".

Robert Fitzhamon had won his lands in Morgannwg by force of arms and, where he had conquered, he enjoyed what amounted to semi-independence from the King. As Lord of Glamorgan, he distributed estates to his loyal followers, dispensed justice and imposed taxes. He and his successors also appear to have retained the chevronels of Iestyn's coat-of-arms though the Clare family, who succeeded to the lordship in the thirteenth century, altered the colour from silver to red and displayed them on a gold background.

For nearly a century, the Clares were one of the most powerful families in the land and Gilbert, the first of his line

OBVERSE.　　　　　　　　　　　　　　REVERSE.

RICHARD DE CLARE, 6TH EARL OF HERTFORD AND GLOUCESTER, 1230—1262.

Seals of the Clare Family, Lords of Glamorgan.　　　*(Cardiff Central Library).*

to become Lord of Glamorgan, was not only a brave crusader but was also one of the principal barons to confront King John at Runnymede, forcing him to sign the Magna Carta. Fifty years later, another Gilbert de Clare, known as the "Red Earl" on account of his auburn hair, played an important role in the affairs of South Wales.

Llywelyn ap Gruffydd, the self-proclaimed Prince of Wales, was rampaging through the Principality. To thwart his ambitions in Glamorgan, the Red Earl built a mighty castle at Caerphilly and then constructed a smaller fortress at Castell Coch to guard the crossing point of the Taff at Tongwynlais. Gilbert now turned his attention to the security of Cardiff. He erected stone walls around the town, most of which survived until the nineteenth century, and strengthened the defences of the castle. To give greater protection to its southern entrance, he built the Black Tower. From this tower he constructed a massive stone wall, complete with guard rooms, to link up with the keep which was also given additional fortifications. This wall was nearly 5 metres high and 2 metres thick and though only the foundations now remain, if you look across the castle green from the keep, you can still appreciate the formidable nature of these mediaeval defences.

9

The male line of the Clare dynasty came to an end at Bannockburn in 1314 when Gilbert III, son of the Red Earl, was killed while fighting for Edward II against the Scots. As one of the great noble families of the realm, the Clares had been deeply involved in affairs of national concern but they had also played a prominent role in the development of Cardiff and for nearly 600 years the chevronels of the Clares became a distinctive feature of the town's coat-of-arms.

Two rampant lions originally supported the shield on the banner but these were replaced when Cardiff became a city. However, the crest and the mural crown, resting on top of a tilting helmet, are part of the borough arms and so is the Tudor Rose, representing the union of the houses of Lancaster and York after the Wars of the Roses. The motto on the crest, "Deffro mae'n ddydd", means "Awake, it is day" and may concern an ancient tale relating to King Arthur. One version of the Arthurian legend names Cardiff as his birthplace and the motto is the call that will arouse Arthur and his knights when Wales has need of them again.

Such was Cardiff's insignia while it remained a borough and one local hostelry, the Cardiff Arms Hotel, not only took its name from the coat-of-arms but proudly displayed the badge above its main entrance. The hotel, which stood at the junction of Castle Street and Westgate Street, was famous as a coaching inn. The first Marquis of Bute provided some of the money to build it and he may have had an ulterior motive as he stayed there on his rare visits to Cardiff, finding it more comfortable than his castle across the road.

For a hundred years, the Cardiff Arms was the place to celebrate a special occasion. In 1794 Lord Mountstuart, heir to the Bute estate, rewarded those voters loyal enough to elect him as their MP with a splendid dinner at the hotel. In 1839 a banquet was held there to mark the opening of the first Bute dock and a year after that directors of the Taff Vale Company invited local dignitaries to join with them in celebrating the completion of the rail link between Cardiff and Merthyr. The hotel continued to flourish until 1882 when it was demolished to allow the construction of Castle Street in its modern form. The hotel may have disappeared

Cardiff Arms Hotel about 1870. *(Cardiff Central Library).*

but the name lives on through the nearby football ground that became the world-famous Cardiff Arms Park.

Two years after Cardiff became a city, the coat-of-arms was changed to reflect its new status. The silver chevronels of Iestyn ap Gwrgant were restored and Edward VII gave permission to incorporate the ostrich feathers of the Prince of Wales in the design. The most interesting additions are the supporters of the shield following a decision to discard the lions rampant in favour of supporters reflecting the place of Cardiff in the modern world.

The seahorse, or hippocamp, on the right represents the Severn Sea, from which a hundred years ago Welsh coal was sent to every corner of the globe. The other supporter is a mountain goat, signifying the hills of Glamorgan where this black wealth was once mined. In 1907 the coal trade was at its zenith and so it is appropriate that Cardiff should recognise its debt to the source of its prosperity and to the outlet which gave it access to the world. Since the goat was also the mascot of the Royal Welsh Regiment of Fusiliers, this is another reason for its presence on the coat-of-arms. The motto below, "Y Ddraig Goch Ddyry Cychwyn" means "The Red Dragon will lead the way" and stresses the city's affinity to Wales.

11

The final additions to the badge were made in 1956 after Cardiff had become the capital of Wales. Each of the supporters was adorned with the Royal Badge of Wales, "an honourable augmentation", or special mark of approval from the Queen, which could only be granted by royal warrant. A quarter of a century ago the coat-of-arms could be seen in the city every day, as it was displayed on all council vehicles, ranging from the humblest dustcart to the Lord Mayor's limousine. This touch of civic pride has gone but, if you go into the Council Chamber at the City Hall, the heraldry of the Welsh capital can be seen in all its finery above the seat where the Lord Mayor presides at council meetings.

The Council Chamber in the City Hall.   *(Dennis Morgan)*.

A HERO OF THE GREAT WAR

In the Gorsedd Gardens, opposite the National Museum, stands the bronze statue of a young officer of the First World War, holding a pair of field glasses as though he is about to spy out the land on the other side of Cathays Park. The inscription on the granite plinth reads,

> "LORD NINIAN EDWARD CRICHTON STUART
> MEMBER OF PARLIAMENT FOR CARDIFF
> COWBRIDGE LLANTRISANT
> LIEUT-COLONEL 6TH BATTALION
> WELSH REG. TERRITORIAL
> BORN 15th MAY 1883
> FELL IN FRANCE AT THE BATTLE OF LOOS
> FIGHTING BRAVELY FOR HIS COUNTRY
> 2nd OCTOBER 1915."

Erected by public subscription, the statue is the work of Sir William Goscombe John who was present at its unveiling on 9 August 1919, nearly four years after Lord Ninian had met his death.

He was born at Dumfries House in Ayrshire and, as the second son of the third Marquis of Bute, he enjoyed all the privileges of belonging to one of the richest and most influential families in Britain. He inherited his father's flair for languages and, after the traditional education for an aristocrat at Harrow and Christchurch, he considered a career in the diplomatic service. Instead he enlisted in the Queen's Own Cameron Highlanders and later served in the Scots Guards. In a tribute to Ninian Stuart after his death, a kinsman recalled, "He thought there was no worthier ambition for a young nobleman than to be a soldier so as to learn discipline, and then to enter the House of Commons to help to manage the affairs of his country".

In 1907 Lord Ninian decided to launch his political career at Cardiff where the local Unionist Party adopted him as their Parliamentary candidate. The seat appeared to be a

Statue of Lord Ninian Stuart.   *(Ian Morgan)*.

forlorn hope for an ambitious Conservative, as Cardiff had consistently returned a Liberal MP, apart from one short break, since 1852. Only the previous year the Liberals had won the constituency by a margin of 3,000, which was a huge majority at that time. Yet from the outset, Lord Ninian held meetings in every ward and worked tirelessly to win over the voters of Cardiff, Cowbridge and Llantrisant. He had been a frequent visitor to Cardiff ever since his childhood, had learnt to speak the Welsh language and was well known in the city because of his family connections. He was not a great public speaker but his courteous, easy manner with people, whatever strata of society they came from, made a favourable impression, even among those who were his political opponents.

Ninian was also fortunate in marrying a lady who worked as tirelessly as he did to promote his political prospects. The Honourable Ismay Lucretia Mary Preston, whom he had married in 1906, made it clear that she was not content to be merely an attractive ornament on the platform beside him. A popular hostess in Society, she now exercised her considerable charm on the voters of Cardiff. When her husband's voice succumbed to the strain of addressing 5 or more meetings a day during the elections of 1910, Lady Ninian was quite happy to speak on his behalf, often with a greater impact.

Ninian Stuart's first opportunity to see if his careful nursing of the seat would yield dividends came in January 1910. On polling day he toured the constituency in his motor car, accompanied by Lady Ninian and their young son who carried a banner with the striking appeal, "Vote for my Daddy". It all proved to be in vain as D.A. Thomas, the Liberal candidate and a prominent figure in the politics of South Wales, won by 1,555 votes. However, the Liberal majority had been halved and Ninian had won a great deal of admiration. He had met what the Tory *Western Mail* called "rude heckling" with good humour, he had won a reputation as, "a downright good sport ... as happy among working men as in a peer's drawing room" and he accepted defeat graciously. He indicated a readiness to fight the seat again and, as events proved, the opportunity came sooner than most people expected.

Spy's Portrait of
Lord Ninian
(Cardiff Castle Collection).

Though the Liberals remained in office after the election, their huge majority of four years earlier was considerably reduced. The great political issue at that time was the reform of the House of Lords and, when George V came to the throne in May 1910, he informed Prime Minister Asquith that he would not accept the Government's proposals until they had been put before the nation a second time. So, in December the Liberal Government was forced to go to the country once again. The result of the election was very similar to that earlier in the year and in due course the reform of the Lords went ahead.

For Lord Ninian, however, the December poll was to be his moment of triumph. He was given encouragement when D.A. Thomas decided to stand down and the Liberals had to choose a fresh candidate, Sir Clarendon Hyde, who knew very little about Cardiff or its politics. Lord Ninian addressed several meetings every day, "enthusiastically seconded by his wife ... whose eloquence and charming presence have added stimulus to the campaign". He made a long list of promises ranging from tariff reform to a strong navy but his principal slogan was, "Remember every vote against Lord Ninian Crichton Stuart is a vote for socialism and unemployment, a vote for the foreigner against the Britisher".

A crowd of 50,000 gathered outside the City Hall on Wednesday 7 December, wearing their colours of Tory blue or Liberal red. The *Western Mail*, partisan as ever, noted that from 9 p.m. "all roads led to Cathays Park ... whence was to be announced the good news that Cardiff had decided for commonsense rather than for madness". The majority was only 299 and, as his opponent observed, the "great personal popularity of Lord Ninian" may have decided the result.

There is no doubt that Ninian Crichton Stuart was well-liked in Cardiff, not least because of the affinity he showed with the community and its interests. He had a reputation as a keen sportsman and in 1910 he helped the Cardiff City Football Club to procure a new ground in Sloper Road. The land was rented from the City Council who required a guarantor for the £90 a year ground rent. His lordship stepped forward to secure the guarantee and in return the club named its new stadium "Ninian Park" in his honour. The official opening of the new ground on 1 September was celebrated with an attractive friendly match against Aston Villa, the Football League Champions. Villa won the game 2-1 but, in a short ceremony before the game began, Lord Ninian wished the club every success and then to resounding cheers kicked off and "set the ball rolling for the City Club in a literal sense".

During his short Parliamentary career, Ninian Stuart was on the opposition benches and had few opportunities to make any impact on the House. Yet he gained a reputation as a champion of all the people he represented and might well have made a name for himself in a future Conservative government. That prize was to be denied him. In 1912 he took command of the 6th Territorial Battalion of the Welsh Regiment which drew its recruits from Swansea and Neath.

Ninian Park, 1910.   *(Richard Shepherd).*

When war broke out in August 1914 the battalion was among the first to leave for France and, in addressing his men before their departure, Lord Ninian said, "I am prepared, as I am sure you all are, to lay down my life for my country if it is required".

A year later these prophetic words came true. During the Battle of Loos, on the afternoon of 2 October 1915, Lieut.-Colonel Stuart was supervising the construction of a communication trench, from a strongpoint known as "Little Willie", towards a new trench. About 3.30 p.m., Little Willie had to be evacuated as a result of intense enemy bombing. When the Germans launched a strike against the new trench, Lord Ninian observed that the Battalion's hand grenade store was becoming a hazard to their safety. It was while urging the men to remove these dangerous weapons that he was fatally shot through the head, dying instantaneously. The Battalion report reads, "He had been the life and soul of the battalion, working for dear life to complete the communication trench and his loss was irreparable". His body, placed in a coffin of zinc and wood, was laid to rest a few days later in the Cave at the public cemetery of Bethune.

Lieut.-Colonel Ninian Stuart. *(Cardiff Castle Collection).*

One of 6 MPs to die in the first World War, Ninian Stuart was sincerely mourned in Cardiff. The *South Wales Daily News*, a political adversary in 1910, recalled his personal charm and the way in which "bitterest political opponents were captivated by the spontaneous and entirely unaffected friendliness of his speech and manner". Similar comments were made on that August afternoon in 1919 when a large gathering witnessed the unveiling of his statue. The Lord Mayor noted that Lord Ninian's last act "was one of self sacrifice on behalf of a friend" and went on to reflect that it was "given to few politicians to enjoy so large a degree of personal popularity or to deserve that popularity so well". It is a fitting epitaph for a man who, though born with a silver spoon in his mouth, believed in a life of service and, if need be, of sacrifice.

Lord Ninian leading his men in the Welsh Regiment 1914.

(Welch Regiment Museum).

ONE OF THE GALLANT SIX HUNDRED

Near the Boulevard de Nantes, facing the City Hall, is a splendid equestrian statue, designed by the famous Cardiff sculptor, Sir William Goscombe John. It shows the figure of the second Viscount Tredegar in the uniform of the XVII Lancers, proudly seated on his horse, Sir Briggs. One of the panels tells us that the statue was, "unveiled on the 55th anniversary of the day when Lord Tredegar, then Captain Godfrey Charles Morgan, lcd a troop of XVII Lancers in the Charge of the Light Brigade at Balaclava". Another panel depicts the famous charge.

The Morgans were one of the leading noble families of South Wales and Godfrey was born at Ruperra Castle in Monmouthshire in 1831. One of his earliest memories was of the Chartist Riots and he later recalled how he was rabbit hunting when the post boy arrived at Ruperra, "pale and quivering", informing him that the streets of Newport were running with blood. Godfrey showed that, even at the age of 8, he had a cool sense of proportion when he told the lad, "Bother your Chartists; come and help me catch this rabbit".

It was in 1853 that Godfrey Morgan enlisted in the army and it was a year later, as a captain in the Lancers, that he took part in the famous charge at Balaclava, immortalised by Tennyson:

> "When will their glory fade?
> Honour the charge they made!
> Honour the Light Brigade,
> Noble Six Hundred".

The Charge of the Light Brigade on 25 October 1854 was one of the great blunders of British military history and Godfrey later recalled the confusion. He maintained the trumpet call to charge was never given and the race towards the Russian guns began on a verbal order which Lord

Statue of Lord Tredegar.   *(Ian Morgan).*

Lord Tredegar in the uniform of the XVII Lancers.   *(Cardiff Central Library).*

Cardigan attempted to reverse. Of the 673 lancers who charged the guns, less than a third survived. The gallantry of the Light Brigade comes out in Godfrey's graphic account of his part in the charge. He describes how he shut his eyes as he saw the Russian gunner applying the fuse only a hundred yards away, "but the shot missed me, and struck the man on my right full in the chest. In another minute I was on the gun and the leading Russian's grey horse ... fell across my horse ... pinning me in between the gun and himself. A Russian gunner, on foot, at once covered me with his carbine. He was just within easy reach of my sword, and I struck him across his neck ... At the same time a mounted gunner struck my horse on the forehead with his sabre. Sir Briggs half jumped, half blundered over the fallen horses and then for a short time bolted with me. I only remember myself alone among the Russians, trying to get out as best I could. This, by some chance, I did, in spite of the attempt of the Russians to cut me down."

Miraculously, the wound to Sir Briggs was the only injury inflicted on either the rider or the horse and it is not difficult to imagine the bond that must have existed between them from this time forth. Sir Briggs lived on for another 20 years and is buried at Tredegar House where a memorial was later erected to him in the Cedar Garden.

Like many men who have experienced death at close quarters, Godfrey Morgan was happy to leave the army soon after the Crimean War ended and for 17 years he served as the Member of Parliament for Breconshire. When his father died in 1875 he became Baron Tredegar and resigned his seat in the Commons, but continued to take an active interest in politics both in the House of Lords and as chairman of the Monmouthshire County Council. His wealth was considerable. Tredegar House, on the outskirts of Newport, was the ancestral home of the Morgan family and the inheritance brought with it estates of more than 40,000 acres. Lord Tredegar also invested over a million pounds in the Alexandra Docks and Railway Company, and his contribution to the development of Newport Docks was as important as that made by the Marquis of Bute to the port of Cardiff.

Godfrey was a natural conservative, not only in politics but also in his way of life. Tredegar House was one of the finest residences in South Wales but no electric or gas lighting were to be found there during his lifetime. Oil lamps and candles were considered to be quite adequate. Nor did he ever really come to terms with other aspects of the

Tredegar House 1995.   *(Dennis Morgan)*.

modern world such as the telephone or "those motor people raising clouds of dust everywhere they go".

Tredegar freely admitted that he had been "blessed with more than his share of this world's goods", but he lived up to the best traditions of the nobility in fulfilling his civic and social duties. The anniversary of the charge at Balaclava was always celebrated with a feast of beef, plum pudding and ale for his tenants and the work-people at Tredegar House. Their feelings towards him are reflected in the words of one of his tenants who admitted, "If I would worship anyone but God it would be Lord Tredegar".

He was a loyal patron of the National Eisteddfod and served for 5 years as President of the University of South Wales and Monmouthshire, contributing more than £13,000 towards its expansion. There are numerous testimonies of his ungrudging support for good causes, most of them in his native Newport where he was described as "a sort of life-president of every public movement". He made gifts to several churches and hospitals in Monmouthshire, including the land on which the Royal Gwent Hospital was built. The attractive open spaces of Belle Vue and Tredegar Park are a legacy of his charity. He was a keen student of archaeology and took a special interest in the excavations which were then in their early stages at Caerwent and Caerleon.

Tredegar was also a liberal benefactor in Cardiff where he owned a considerable amount of land west of the River Rhymney. He contributed thousands of pounds to the Royal Infirmary and provided sites for a number of churches, among them St. German's, St. James's in Newport Road and Tredegarville Baptist Church. When Albany Road, Penylan Hill and Newport Road were widened, he told the city engineer to take whatever land was required for this purpose free of charge. A few years earlier, in 1894, he offered 5 acres of land towards the creation of Roath Park, while a short distance away the gift of Roath Brook Gardens, Roath Mill Gardens and Waterloo Gardens resulted in a beautiful stretch of greenery from Penylan to Newport Road. In Splott, Lord Tredegar not only donated the land on which the park and the library were built, but also gave away a further 30 acres to provide allotments for the local people.

Such generosity explains why Lord Tredegar was so highly regarded both in his native Monmouthshire and in Glamorgan. Honours were showered upon him in his later life. In 1905 he became a viscount and in December 1907 the county of Monmouthshire presented him with a gold

Waterloo Gardens 1995. *(Ian Morgan)*

cup, a portrait in oils of himself and an album containing the names of 7,000 people who had subscribed to these gifts. A further £2,000 in cash was left untouched and it is characteristic of Tredegar that he donated this money to the hospitals of the county.

In 1909 the Viscount was awarded the freedom of Newport. Later that year, on the anniversary of the Charge of the Light Brigade, it was the turn of Cardiff and Glamorgan to show their appreciation of this old warrior, now 78 years of age. The ceremony and presentation of a gilded casket containing the scroll of the freedom of Cardiff took place at the City Hall. It was a bright, crisp October day and after lunch the equestrian statue, a tribute from the county of Glamorgan, was unveiled by the Earl of Plymouth, who said, "Soldier, sportsman, country gentleman and philanthropist, Lord Tredegar is a man who embodies all that is best in the character of his race". The Welsh Regiment provided a guard of honour for the ceremony and a poignant touch was added to the occasion by the presence of 20 survivors from the Crimean War. The bronze statue, which had cost £4,000, was Goscombe John's first attempt at equine sculpture. Both man and horse, he said, were meant to display "an arrested alertness ... and my desire was that

Unveiling
Lord Tredegar's
Statue,
25 October 1909.
*(Cardiff Central
Library)*.

both of them should appear as animated as possible, as i
ready to start at the slightest word of command".

Tredegar genuinely believed that great personal wealth
carried with them the obligations of social responsibility. He
had a jovial, easy-going manner that earned him the title of
"The Mark Twain of the Peerage" and such words as, "frank
light-hearted and approachable" were often applied to him
After a lengthy illness, Godfrey died on 11 March 1913 at
the age of 81. He never married and within half a century the
family line came to an end. His remains were laid to rest in
Bassaleg Church, a short distance from Tredegar House
now in the process of being tastefully restored through the
efforts of the Newport Borough Council. It had been the
home of the Morgans for more than 500 years and it is
probably true to say that no member of that family was more
popular than Godfrey, the hero of Balaclava who was spared
in that dreadful slaughter to become a generous and much
loved benefactor to the people of Monmouthshire and
Glamorgan.

Lord Tredegar
inspecting the South
Wales Scouts with
Lord Baden-Powell
1910.
*(Cardiff Central
Library).*

THE ROMAN FORT

This plaque, placed at the main entrance to Cardiff Castle, is in a bilingual form and from it we learn that 4 Roman forts once occupied this site. Yet, little more than a hundred years ago, our knowledge of the Roman presence in Cardiff was very scanty indeed. A lofty, grassy bank surrounded the perimeter of the castle and, while it bore some resemblance to the shape of a Roman fort, archaeologists could not understand why the Romans had not built in stone as they usually did. In fact, the stone wall was discovered by accident in 1889, when the third Marquis of Bute gave orders to slice through the bank so that he could construct a passageway from the castle to his garden in Cathays Park. Imagine the excitement and astonishment when the workmen uncovered a huge mass of masonry. Fortunately, the Marquis was a keen archaeologist and he ensured that the site was properly excavated. When Duke Street was widened in 1923, the Fourth Marquis of Bute reconstructed the walls and the North Gate in their original form, a restoration that is widely accepted as one of the best examples of how a

The Roman Wall from Duke Street 1995.   *(Ian Morgan).*

ROMAN FORTS OF CARDIFF

This area of Cardiff was occupied by units of the Roman Army almost continually from the first until the fourth century. The first fort was a large frontier base established in the mid-first century and occupied until about 75AD. This was replaced by a smaller fort occupying the northern half of the present castle enclosure and beyond. The second fort was rebuilt at least once, before being replaced, in the mid-third century, by a fort, the lower walls of which formed the basis for the present 19th and 20th century reconstruction.

Bu unedau o'r Fyddin Rufeinig yn bresennol yn y rhan hon o Gaerdydd yn gyson rhwng y ganrif gyntaf a'r bedwaredd ganrif. Gwersyll ffin sylweddol oedd y gaer gyntaf a sefydlwyd ar ganol y ganrif gyntaf ai defnyddio hyd tua 75 OC. Disodlwyd hon gan gaer lai a fodolai yn hanner ogleddol cyntedd presennol y Castell a thu hwnt. Ailadeiladwyd yr ail gaer o leiaf unwaith, cyn i gaer arall gymryd ei lle ar ganol y drydedd ganrif, Llunia muriau isaf hon seiliau'r atgynhyrchiad presennol a ddyddia o'r 19eg a'r 20fed ganrif.

(23)

RHODD DINAS CAERDYDD, TACHWEDD 1993
DONATED BY THE CITY OF CARDIFF, NOVEMBER 1993

Plaque of the Roman Forts at Cardiff Castle.   *(Ian Morgan)*

Roman fort would have appeared. More recent excavations have revealed that the present fort was the fourth to be built on the site.

About 50AD South Wales was occupied by the Silures, a tribe of fierce warriors who gave themselves an even more ferocious appearance by painting themselves with woad before going into battle. Inside the Roman wall today you can see a graphic portrayal by Frank Abrahams of the manner in which the Silures lived and of how they attempted to repel the Roman invaders who subdued them in a methodically planned campaign. Vessels, patrolling the Bristol Channel, carefully observed every movement the Silures made along the coast, while inland Roman soldiers systematically built roads and forts as they advanced into Wales.

Within 5 years a major fortress at Usk was providing accommodation for the Twentieth Legion under its commander, Didius Gallus, and it was about this time that the Romans built their first fort at Cardiff. They chose the site as it was an important river crossing and, since the ground level was much lower in those days than it is now, the fort also served as a naval base to strengthen their control of the Bristol Channel.

One of the murals in the Roman Wall, depicting the struggle between the Romans and the Silures. *(Ian Morgan).*

This first fort or castrum, as the plaque tells us, was much larger than the present site. In modern terms its area stretched approximately from the Angel Hotel to Queenswest and from there to the Law Courts and Bute Park. Gates at the northern and southern entrances were made from timber but otherwise the fortifications were no more than high banks of earth. Inside the fort, apart from the usual barracks, stores and workshops, traces have been discovered of a timber-framed house which was probably the private quarters of the commander. The castrum existed to extend Roman power and influence throughout the region and, since it was not equipped to withstand a lengthy siege, the conquerors obviously regarded this eventuality as unlikely.

However, their campaign against the Silures was temporarily halted by the revolt of Boadicea in Eastern Britain but, after crushing that rebellion, the Romans completed the conquest of South Wales. A new headquarters at Caerleon replaced the legionary fortress at Usk and a chain of forts was built along the coast, linked by military roads along which an army could march up to 60 miles a day in the event of a crisis.

The most belligerent Silurian warrior bowed to the inevitable and, for nearly two centuries, South Wales enjoyed the benefits of the Pax Romana. Merchant ships from every part of the Empire became a familiar sight in the Bristol Channel, laden with cargoes of Samian pottery, beakers made in Lyons, or wine from Italy and Gaul. Elegant marble from Greece or Italy was imported to build the splendid villas at Llantwit Major, Dinas Powys and Ely.

In this peaceful era, the fort at Cardiff was greatly reduced in size. The northern boundary remained unchanged but, in a modern context, the southern bank stretched across the Castle Green from the Norman keep to the east wall. A civil settlement grew up to the south of the fort and traces of slag, found in recent excavations, indicate that iron smelting was a local industry. The remains of long, rectangular buildings were also found and when Lloyd's Bank was built in High Street, coins and pottery from this little community were discovered. By 165 the region was so peaceful that most forts in Glamorgan were abandoned and the castrum at Cardiff was scaled down even further.

The Pax Romana began to disintegrate in the third century as barbarians began to attack the Empire from all quarters. To meet the threat from Irish pirates who raided and plundered the villas and country districts of South Wales ever more boldly, the Romans strengthened their defences along the coast. The fort at Cardiff was vital in this respect and about 250 it was rebuilt on its present site.

Sturdy walls of stone were built for the first time, the construction of which can be fully appreciated when you visit the Roman wall inside the castle. The outer face of the wall, best seen from Duke Street, is 17 feet high and is lined with dressed limestone that was probably obtained from the cliffs near Aberthaw. Smaller pebbles, taken from the river and grouted with mortar, gave great strength to the core of the wall which, at its base, is over 10 feet thick. When the interior facing wall, also built of limestone, reaches a height of 9 feet, the thickness is gradually reduced in stages until at the summit it is no more than 5 1/2 feet. Embankments of soil gave additional strength to the walls inside the fort, while polygon bastions bonded to the wall provided firing platforms for ballista and giant catapults. We can gauge

The Roman North Gate, shortly after excavation, 1900.

(Cardiff Central Library).

some idea of the durability of Roman craftmanship when we remember that the wall acted as an air raid shelter for the people of Cardiff in the Second World War.

There were 2 gates into the fort. The water gate at the southern entrance is no longer visible, though its remains still lie under the ramp by which modern visitors approach the castle. When the North Gate was re-discovered in 1889, approximately 5 feet of the original masonry survived which served as a base for its re-construction in 1923. Meticulous attention was paid to detail and even the bridge across the moat in Bute Park is designed along Roman lines.

It is difficult to draw firm conclusions about the interior of the fort. The slag heaps of the iron smelters probably became the foundations for the timber barracks, cookhouses, storerooms and latrines, common to all Roman forts. One interesting discovery was made in 1777 when a hypocaust was found in the south-west corner of the castle. It was almost certainly a feature of the indoor baths that were built in the final Roman fort at Cardiff.

During the last years of the Roman occupation, the castrum probably resembled a small fortified town, offering some shelter against marauding pirates. Supplies were unloaded from quays along the river but in the end all these efforts to provide a safe haven came to nought, as the legions were withdrawn to defend Rome itself. The local people took to the hills for safety as the walls crumbled and the wooden barracks rotted. Yet Cardiff's name originates from the Roman occupation for, though there are differing opinions about the placename, most authorities agree it refers to "the fortress by the river".

The site was probably never completely deserted from this time forth but it ceased to be of major importance until the Normans conquered Glamorgan at the end of the eleventh century. In 1080 William the Conqueror is said to have passed through Cardiff on a pilgrimage to St. David's and ordered a castle to be built within the Roman ruins, but nothing was done until Robert Fitzhamon conquered Glamorgan some years later. He certainly appreciated the

Left: Cardiff Castle and the Roman Fort in the 1920's.*(Cardiff Central Library).*

strategic possibilities of the old fort and built a wooden motte and bailey castle within its ruined walls. It was his successors, the mediaeval lords of Glamorgan, who covered the walls with great banks of earth, 27 feet high, thus ensuring that the secrets of Roman Cardiff disappeared into the mists of time until that exciting discovery in 1889.

THE NORTH GATE AND
THE TOWN WALLS

A plaque, marking the site of the mediaeval North Gate, is fixed to the wall of the Northgate building in Kingsway. At the rear of the Queenswest shopping centre nearby, another plaque reminds us of the wall that once surrounded Cardiff. It is difficult to determine when the town walls were first built but the earliest mention of them is to be found in the *Brut y Tywysogion*, written by the Welsh chronicler, Caradoc of Llancarfan. He refers to a timber palisade, pierced by 4 openings, which was built around "the fortified town of Cardiff" in 1111. These entrances were to become the main gateways into the mediaeval borough.

Two gatekeepers, who were employed to open and close the gates every morning and evening, were paid the princely sum of 2d a day for carrying out their duties, though they were also allowed to live rent-free above the West and North Gates. When the bells of St. John's Church rang out to announce the beginning of the day, it was the gatekeepers' duty to open all the town gates for business. Likewise, the bells pealed out each evening to signal the curfew and the closing of the gates, after which law-abiding folk were expected to be within their homes. The walls were not only intended to offer a protection against an attack from the turbulent Welsh, still nursing resentment against their Anglo-Norman conquerors, but also played an important role in maintaining law and order. Cardiff was then a small town of about 2,000 people who all knew one another and regarded any strangers with suspicion. While "foreigners" were tolerated in the day-time, at night the gates were a means of keeping unwelcome intruders out of the town.

When the borough was first granted its charter, the gates had a further purpose since they were a means of controlling commercial activity in and out of the town. The lords of Glamorgan absolved all merchants and craftsmen in Cardiff from paying any tolls on their goods but the levying of tolls

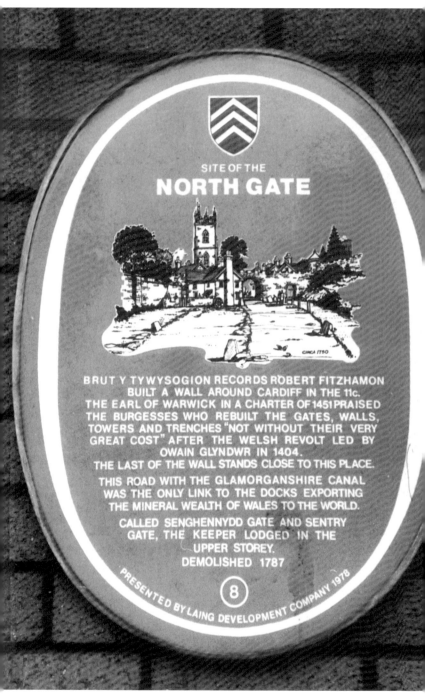

SITE OF THE
NORTH GATE

BRUT Y TYWYSOGION RECORDS ROBERT FITZHAMON
BUILT A WALL AROUND CARDIFF IN THE 11c.
THE EARL OF WARWICK IN A CHARTER OF 1451 PRAISED
THE BURGESSES WHO REBUILT THE GATES, WALLS,
TOWERS AND TRENCHES "NOT WITHOUT THEIR VERY
GREAT COST" AFTER THE WELSH REVOLT LED BY
OWAIN GLYNDWR IN 1404.
THE LAST OF THE WALL STANDS CLOSE TO THIS PLACE.

THIS ROAD WITH THE GLAMORGANSHIRE CANAL
WAS THE ONLY LINK TO THE DOCKS EXPORTING
THE MINERAL WEALTH OF WALES TO THE WORLD.

CALLED SENGHENNYDD GATE AND SENTRY
GATE, THE KEEPER LODGED IN THE
UPPER STOREY.
DEMOLISHED 1787

(8)

PRESENTED BY LAING DEVELOPMENT COMPANY 1978

Plaque of the Town North Gate. *(Ian Morgan).*

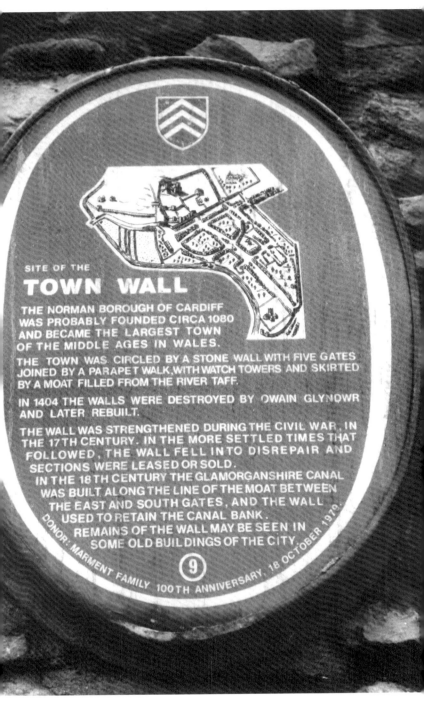

SITE OF THE

TOWN WALL

THE NORMAN BOROUGH OF CARDIFF WAS PROBABLY FOUNDED CIRCA 1080 AND BECAME THE LARGEST TOWN OF THE MIDDLE AGES IN WALES.

THE TOWN WAS CIRCLED BY A STONE WALL WITH FIVE GATES JOINED BY A PARAPET WALK, WITH WATCH TOWERS AND SKIRTED BY A MOAT FILLED FROM THE RIVER TAFF.

IN 1404 THE WALLS WERE DESTROYED BY OWAIN GLYNDWR AND LATER REBUILT.

THE WALL WAS STRENGTHENED DURING THE CIVIL WAR, IN THE 17TH CENTURY. IN THE MORE SETTLED TIMES THAT FOLLOWED, THE WALL FELL INTO DISREPAIR AND SECTIONS WERE LEASED OR SOLD.

IN THE 18TH CENTURY THE GLAMORGANSHIRE CANAL WAS BUILT ALONG THE LINE OF THE MOAT BETWEEN THE EAST AND SOUTH GATES, AND THE WALL USED TO RETAIN THE CANAL BANK.

REMAINS OF THE WALL MAY BE SEEN IN SOME OLD BUILDINGS OF THE CITY.

DONOR: MARMENT FAMILY 100TH ANNIVERSARY, 18 OCTOBER 1979.

(9)

Plaque of the Town Wall.   *(Ian Morgan).*

Kingsway 1995. *(Ian Morgan).*

on strangers wishing to trade in the market place was a lucrative source of income. Furthermore the gates allowed the officers of the Town Guild to check whether a stranger was trying to set up an illegal business within the community, for any competition of this kind was not tolerated in a society where restrictive practices were common and consumer rights virtually unknown.

At the end of the thirteenth century when Llywelyn, the last Welsh Prince of Gwynedd, was rampaging through Wales, the Lord of Glamorgan decided to strengthen the defences of his most important borough by rebuilding the walls and gates in stone. The North Gate was one of 6 built by Gilbert de Clare and it was better known among local people as "Porth Senghenydd". It gained its name from the area to the north of Cardiff near Caerphilly which, for a hundred years or more after the Norman invasion, still displayed an independent defiance towards the conquerors of Glamorgan.

Gradually the lords of Senghenydd were forced to recognise the Normans as their overlords but they still held the right to govern their territory according to Welsh custom and law. This uneasy truce held until 1158 when Earl William decided it was time to end any privileges of this sort and using, Norman law, he seized land belonging to Ifor ap Meurig, the Lord of Senghennydd. William stirred up a hornets' nest for no-one typified the smouldering resentment of the Welsh better than Ifor Bach who, despite his small stature, possessed a fiery temper. He decided it was time to teach this arrogant Norman a lesson he would not forget. Ifor and a small band of warriors rode down to Cardiff and tied up their horses just outside the North Gate. It is not clear how they penetrated the castle defences but probably they were helped by some-one inside the castle. Perhaps the gate was left open or maybe the castle guards were drugged. Of one thing we can be certain. It must have been an awful shock for William and his wife when Ifor burst into their personal chambers and carried them off with their young son to Senghennydd where he dictated his own peace terms.

This daring coup occurred before Gilbert fortified the town defences but even the new walls and gates were no guarantee against a determined assault. In 1316 Llywelyn Bren, a descendant of Ifor Bach, stormed through the town walls and besieged the castle. Eventually he was forced to withdraw and a powerful royal army of more than 2,000 men was assembled at Cardiff to quell the rebellion. On 12 March 1316 the King's forces marched out of the North Gate and caught up with Llywelyn at Castell Morgraig, the ruins of which still stand near the Travellers' Rest on Caerphilly Mountain. The Welshmen were routed and Llywelyn was captured soon afterwards. In due course he suffered the terrible death of a traitor and was hung from the Black Tower at Cardiff Castle before his body was cut down, drawn and quartered as a warning to other rebels.

The Rose and Crown public house can be found near the plaque commemorating the North Gate. An earlier pub of the same name stood here and served as a coaching inn for travellers to Merthyr, but it was certainly not the most healthy place in Cardiff to buy a drink. Not far away, one of the town's dunghills gave off an evil stench and, whenever it rained heavily, the revolting slurry was washed down into the yard of the pub.

Not far from the North Gate, where Kingsway and Queen Street now meet, people gathered to watch the barbarous pastime of bull baiting. The bull was tethered to a long rope and mastiffs were released into the ring, two or three at a time, to launch themselves upon the poor beast. Some of the dogs would be killed but if a mastiff succeeded in fastening its teeth into the nose of the bull, nothing would shake it off.

The Rose and Crown Public House 1913. *(Fred Jones)*

The North Gate 1776 by Paul Sandby. *(Cardiff Central Library)*

A coroner's report of 1773 relates how a spectator strayed too close to the bull and was gored to death. This was a cruel age and such sport as bull baiting and cock fighting were common. Indeed the Council encouraged these pastimes as the Corporation accounts during the eighteenth century show regular payments to wash the bull's collar or to purchase a new rope.

Looking towards the North Gate and St. John's Church was a popular theme for artists of the eighteenth century and Sandby's view of 1775 gives a realistic impression of the highway at that time. The wall of the friary can be seen on the left, while to the right is an open view of the castle, reflecting a tranquillity so very different from the hectic flow of traffic in Kingsway today. A similar scene is portrayed on the mural outside Marks and Spencers store in the St. David's shopping centre.

The walls and gates of Cardiff remained intact until the end of the eighteenth century, by which time they were becoming an obstacle to traffic and had outlived their protective role. The North Gate was among the first to be demolished in 1787 and, as Cardiff expanded throughout the next hundred years, the mediaeval walls were pulled down without any attempt to preserve them. Until recently, most people in Cardiff had forgotten they ever existed but the erection of the blue plaques has given a belated recognition of their historical importance.

SITE OF THE
EAST GATE

PART OF THE NORMAN DEFENCES OF THE TOWN.
THROUGH THIS GATE CAME ALL WHO TRAVELLED THE
ANCIENT ROAD BETWEEN GLOUCESTER AND SWANSEA.
KNOWN AS PORTH CROCKERTON, FROM THE DISTRICT
OF CROCKHERBTOWN, POSSIBLY NAMED FOR THE FINE
VEGETABLE GARDENS OF THE 13TH CENTURY HOUSE
OF THE GREYFRIARS, CLOSE BY.
THE TOWN HOSPICE STOOD OUTSIDE THIS GATE.
RESTORED AFTER THE WELSH UPRISING OF 1404
THE FORTIFIED TRIPLE ARCHED STONE GATEWAY,
WITH SENTRY AND SLOPE HOUSES, WAS
DEMOLISHED IN 1781 TO IMPROVE THE TOLL ROAD.
IN THE 18TH CENTURY WITH THE BUILDING OF
THE GLAMORGANSHIRE CANAL,
CROCKHERBTOWN LOCK STOOD BY THE
SITE OF THE OLD GATE.
AT THE TURN OF THE CENTURY
THIS PLACE WAS STILL KNOWN AS
"THE PILLARS".

6

DONATED BY B.H.S. LTD. OCTOBER 1977

Plaque of the East Gate.   *(Ian Morgan).*

THE EAST GATE

This plaque on the wall of Queenswest commemorates the mediaeval gateway into Cardiff from the east. In front of the shopping centre, a broad band of black and red stones, stretching across the road, marks the site of the East Gate, while the openings between the stones represent the entrances into the town for traffic and pedestrians.

Today, Queen Street is Cardiff's busiest shopping area but in the Middle Ages the district was known as Crockerton or Crockherbtown, and it lay outside the East Gate to which local people gave the name, "Porth Crockerton". As early as 1171, Cardiff was beginning to sprawl beyond its walls and William, Lord of Glamorgan, was proudly referring to "my new borough which I have made ... outside the town of Cardiff". It appears that Crockherbtown gained its name from the local custom of selling fruit, herbs and vegetables in china dishes or crocks, though the plaque also mentions that this unusual name might be derived from the gardens of the Greyfriars Convent which lay a short distance north of

Outline of the
Town Wall
at Queenswest.
(Ian Morgan).

45

the East Gate. In 1887 Crockerton Street was renamed Queen Street to mark the occasion of Queen Victoria's Golden Jubilee. It was a decision that caused some resentment at the time and a petition, signed by many local residents, regretted, "that so well known and ancient a name, which has distinguished this respectable part of Cardiff from time immemorial, should be abolished". Now the only reminder of this ancient district of Cardiff is Crockherbtown Lane, the rather dingy alleyway that runs parallel with Queen Street from Park Place.

For hundreds of years the East Gate was a very busy place in Cardiff. Every day, until the mid-nineteenth century, crowds gathered at the gate to use the Crockerton pump that was said to provide the best drinking water in the town, though unfortunately demand was so great that the pump invariably ran dry by evening. Twice a week, on Wednesdays and Saturdays, farmers from Roath and Rumney passed through the East Gate to sell their produce at the market held in High Street. In June and September the population of Cardiff became swollen many times over as crowds flocked through the gate to visit and trade at the annual fairs which were held to celebrate the feasts of St. John and St. Mary.

The East Gate was dismantled in 1781 after shopkeepers and traders grumbled that it was causing traffic congestion but the arches of the gate remained standing for some time afterwards. These arches were known locally as "The Pillars", a name that has been adopted by a restaurant a short distance away in Queen Street. Despite the disappearance of the East Gate, the area continued to be one of the busiest in the town. Not far away from "The Pillars", John Bradley distributed the mail from Cardiff's earliest post office in Smith Street. He was not only the town's postmaster but also had a lucrative business as a coach proprietor, and it was his responsibility to collect the letters and packages from the London coach as it pulled up outside the Angel Inn opposite the castle. The mail coach always attracted a large crowd, eager to hear the latest gossip from the capital. The coachman, resplendent in his top hat; the horses, bedecked in beautiful ribbons; and the guard, magnificent in his scarlet

Queenswest Shopping Centre 1995. *(Ian Morgan).*

coat as he blew his gleaming horn to announce his arrival; all contributed to a colourful spectacle.

Within a few years of the demolition of the East Gate, another landmark had taken its place. In the late eighteenth century the Industrial Revolution had transformed Merthyr into the "Iron Capital" of the world. With an abundance of limestone, iron ore and coal, the region had all the natural resources it required for the making of good quality iron. The only facility lacking was an adequate transport system for the finished product and to fulfil this need the iron masters decided to build the Glamorganshire canal from Merthyr to Cardiff. Work began in 1790 and the enterprise was a wonderful feat of engineering as navvies, working with picks and shovels, carved out 26 miles of waterway in only 8 years. Along the route, nearly 50 locks were constructed to counteract the 568 feet drop in elevation and, until the coming of the railway and the building of the first dock, the canal remained the major highway linking Cardiff with the valleys.

In the 1830's more than 200 barges were using the canal day and night. The little narrow boats became a familiar sight as the horses plodded along the towpaths of

Weighbridge of the Glamorganshire Canal at Crockherbtown. *(National Museum of*

Whitchurch, Llandaff North and Gabalfa into Cardiff. As the canal entered the town, it followed the route of the mediaeval moat along the castle wall. The pedestrian underpass a Kingsway is one of the few visible traces of the canal tha still remains, for it was here that the barges would carefully negotiate the narrow tunnel under the road before wending their way along The Friary to the weighbridge a Crockherbtown.

The weighbridge, just a few metres away from the site o: the East Gate, was a beehive of activity. The barges were lifted out of the water into a cradle and weighed so that the tolls could be calculated. Heavy goods, such as coal, sand o iron were charged at a rate of 2d per ton per mile and genera merchandise at 5d per ton per mile. In 1894 this weighbridge was moved to North Road where it was a familiar landmark until after the Second World War. Sixty years later, when the canal was filled in, the Council had no use for this memento from Cardiff's past and today, if you want to see the old Crockerton weighbridge, you have to visit the Stoke Bruerne Waterways Museum in Northamptonshire.

After each vessel was weighed, the bargee used a boat-hook to propel himself through a tunnel 100 metres long

Masons' Arms Hotel before the First World War.

(Cardiff Central Library).

Queen Street Chambers 1995. *(Ian Morgan).*

This is now covered by the Queens Arcade but next door to the arcade is a nineteenth century building with a most interesting Venetian architectural style, which was almost certainly intended to blend into the background of the canal and represents another connection with its past.

In 1792 the Masons' Arms public house was built near the weighbridge. This tavern, popular with visitors entering Cardiff from the east, survived until 1911 when it was demolished and replaced with the Carlton Rooms. For many years this fine three-storey building was a popular rendezvous for a meal in the restaurant or an afternoon tea dance with music provided by the Carlton Orchestra. For the less musically inclined there were 22 billiard tables to provide an alternative form of entertainment. The Carlton flourished until the building was severely damaged in an air raid on 3 March 1941. Attempts to re-establish the Carlton failed after the war and the music of the thirties became a distant memory as the site was first of all occupied by the British Home Stores and later by the Queenswest shopping centre. The canal itself continued to be used until the Second World War and the decision to fill it in, taken by the council some years afterwards, certainly lacked imagination as the canal would now have made a wonderful link between the town and Cardiff Bay.

THE CROCKHERBTOWN THEATRE

The plaque on the Nationwide Building Society in Queen Street tells us that the Theatre Royal, the first proper theatre to open its doors in Cardiff, was built on this site. There had been earlier makeshift playhouses in Quay Street, Trinity Street and near the workhouse in St. Mary Street, but they were little better than barns, offering performances only at irregular intervals. However, in September 1825 a company of local gentlemen encouraged by Mrs. Wyndham Lewis, the future wife of Benjamin Disraeli, placed an advertisement in the local press offering a payment of £10 for "the best plan and estimate for the theatre to be built at Cardiff". The frontage was not to exceed 40 feet and a limit of £1,200 was placed on the building costs. Three trustees were appointed to supervise the project, one of whom was John Bird whose diary tells us that plans and proposals to commence building work were approved on 25 January 1826.

The theatre was built near Bradley's Lane which took its name from the fine house on the corner, owned by William Bradley, an hereditary freeman of Cardiff. J. Pitt Hardacre, reminiscing about his acting career at the Theatre Royal,

The Crockherbtown Theatre and Bradley's House.   *(Mr. & Mrs. B.J. Weston)*.

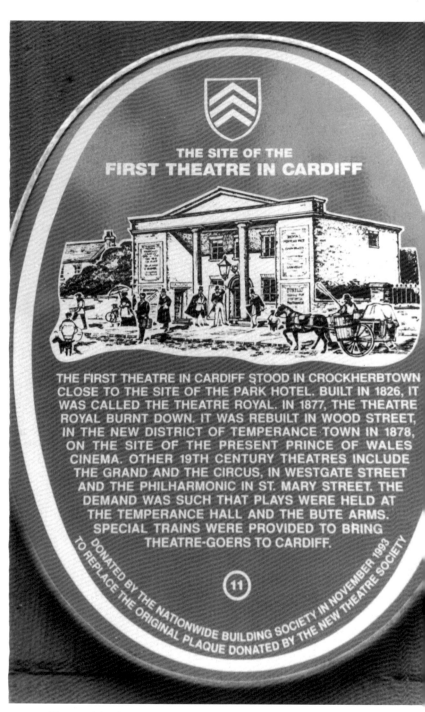

THE SITE OF THE
FIRST THEATRE IN CARDIFF

THE FIRST THEATRE IN CARDIFF STOOD IN CROCKHERBTOWN CLOSE TO THE SITE OF THE PARK HOTEL. BUILT IN 1826, IT WAS CALLED THE THEATRE ROYAL. IN 1877, THE THEATRE ROYAL BURNT DOWN. IT WAS REBUILT IN WOOD STREET, IN THE NEW DISTRICT OF TEMPERANCE TOWN IN 1878, ON THE SITE OF THE PRESENT PRINCE OF WALES CINEMA. OTHER 19TH CENTURY THEATRES INCLUDE THE GRAND AND THE CIRCUS, IN WESTGATE STREET AND THE PHILHARMONIC IN ST. MARY STREET. THE DEMAND WAS SUCH THAT PLAYS WERE HELD AT THE TEMPERANCE HALL AND THE BUTE ARMS. SPECIAL TRAINS WERE PROVIDED TO BRING THEATRE-GOERS TO CARDIFF.

(11)

DONATED BY THE NATIONWIDE BUILDING SOCIETY IN NOVEMBER 1993 TO REPLACE THE ORIGINAL PLAQUE DONATED BY THE NEW THEATRE SOCIETY

Plaque of the Crockherbtown Theatre.   *(Ian Morgan).*

remembered a "peculiar little building", separated from Bradley's house by a pretty garden that led to the stage door. Public excitement grew as the auditorium, capable of holding 1,000 people, took shape. The local press also waxed lyrical, observing that "Old Cardiff ... almost lost its head with delight when it viewed the swelling outlines and pretentious proportions of the Crockherbtown theatre".

Each subscriber, who purchased one of the £25 shares issued by the company, was given a silver ticket which ensured free admission to any performance at any time. Presumably all shareholders were in attendance for the opening night at the theatre on 5 September 1827 when a performance of *The Honeymoon* was followed by a farce with a "brilliant assemblage". Paying customers were charged 3/- for admission to a box, 2/- for a seat in the pit and a mere 1/- to sit on the hard benches in the gallery.

Despite the enthusiasm of the local people for this new venture, its commercial prospects were less rosy, especially in the first few years after it opened. One local resident, looking back to those early days, commented that the investors who had put their money into the building of the Theatre Royal "did not care much about its being a paying concern - or if they did they were disappointed". William

Crockherbtown 1840 - the Theatre is on the right.   *(Cardiff Central Library)*.

Bird, in his *Guide to Cardiff* for 1829, wrote gloomily, "the pit, being very much below the level of the road, is constantly flooded in wet seasons, and the property is, in consequence, almost useless". For several years flooding after heavy rain was a real problem, though mischievous lads had a grand time, sailing on planks in the flooded area while waving their arms about in an attempt to imitate real actors. This particular problem was solved in 1836 when the dock feeder, which was being excavated to supply the West Dock, passed by the eastern side of the theatre and drained away any water that had infiltrated the pit.

The dressing room overlooked the feeder which proved to be very convenient for one member of Mr. Hardacre's company. This particular actor, known as "Puggy" Watson on account of his prominent nose, brought his rod and line with him to the theatre and, when he was not on stage, he lit his pipe and relaxed with a little fishing from his dressing room window. Many times the owners of the theatre must have blessed the dock feeder since, apart from draining the pit, it could also be used to clean the scenery. When the management felt it was time for a new set, they washed the canvases in what was then reasonably clean water before painting them with a new background.

Perhaps "Puggy" was justified in enjoying his offstage rest periods for the audiences of those days could be very intimidating. The gallery, known as the "Lions' Den" on account of the railings that enclosed the front, was particularly raucous. If the band was a little late in striking up the overture, the "lions" would usually target the Italian bass player with the cry, "Play up Italy", before hurling orange peel and anything else that came to hand at the rest of the orchestra. To rub salt in the wound, many of the lads in the gallery never paid for admission. One of them would buy a 6d ticket and then remove a few slates from the roof, while his cronies climbed up the drain pipe and gained unofficial entry from above. The practice, known as "taking a roof ticket", was only detected when the lighting failed one evening and the spectators were offered a refund. The lads who had gained free entry claimed their 6d rebate alongside the rest of the audience, and so the management was left to

THEATRE, CARDIFF.

BY AUTHORITY.

FOR THE BENEFIT OF

MR. BRAID.

ON FRIDAY EVENING, 26th NOVEMBER, 1841,

The Performances will commence with the Favorite Comedy, of

THE

WONDER;

A Woman Keeps a Secret.

Don Felix..Mr. T GREEN. | Don Lopez..Mr. LECLERCQ. | Frederick..Mr. H. FRAZER. | Col. Briton....Mr. BRAID.
Don Pedro..Mr. MULFORD, | Gibby..Mr. ARTAUD. | Lissardo..Mr. W. H. ANGEL.... | Alguazil..Mr. YOUNG.
Vasquez..................Mr. REDFERN | Sancho....................Mr. KIMBER.
Violante....Miss ELLIS. | Isabella...Mrs. LECLERCQ. | Inis....Mrs. W. H. ANGEL. | Flora......Mrs. G. NORMAN.

AN ADMIRED SONG, BY MR. REDFERN.

To conclude with the peculiar and popular Drama, of

VICTORINE,

THE ORPHAN OF PARIS;

OR, I'LL SLEEP ON IT.

No piece in Paris, during the last Ten years, has made a stronger impression than that of "VICTORINE," of which the above is an adaption.—The simplicity of the story, the powerful interest of the situations, the ingenuity of the construction, and above all, the strong and obvious moral lesson it conveys, are all titles to excellence which eminently merit a transfer to the English Stage.

ACT. 1.	ACT. 2.	ACT. 3.
Scene.—Mansarde of Victorine, in Rue St Honoré.	A supposed lapse of five years, has occurred since the First Act.	A supposed lapse of 20 years, has occurred since the Second Act.
Alexandré(a Roue)aged 35. Mr. Braid.	Alexandré (a Horse Dealer) aged 40....	Alexandre,(a Juggler and escaped convict) aged 60 ....Mr. Braid.
Michael(an upholsterer)aged 2'.......	........................Mr. Braid.	Chanteloupe(his companion, an old Soldier)
Victorine(an Embroidress) aged 19......	Michael (an Upholsterer) aged 25....	........................Mr. Silver.
........................Miss Ellis.	........................Mr. H. Frazer.	Mr. Bonassus (a Widower) aged 55...
Elise (a Sempstress) aged 20..........	Madame St. Victor aged 24 . .Miss Ellis.	........................Mr. W. H. Angel.
........................Mr .G. Norman.	Madame le Baronne Elise, aged 25	Blaise (his Valet) aged 40. .Mr Artaud.
	........................Mrs.G. Norman.	Michael (a Cap. of the National Guards) aged 40 ....Mr. H. Frazer.
	Justine, Femme de Chambre to Madame St. Victor.........Mrs. Hutchins.	Barnard (a Silversmith)....Mr Kimber.
	Mr. Bonassus aged 35. . Mr W .H. Angel.	Victorine (a Eating House Keeper) aged
	Blaise (his man,)aged 20. Mr Artaud.	........................44 Miss Ellis.
	Macaire (friend of Alexandre)Mr Young.	Elise (a Vender of Oranges) aged 45....
	Mrs. Bonassus ......Mrs. Macnamara.	........................Mrs. G. Norman
		Sophie ....Miss Jones.

Tickets and Places for the Boxes, to be had of Mr. Braid, at the White Lion Inn, Castle Street ; and at the Post-Office.

Doors open at half past Six, Performance to commence at Seven —BOXES, 3s.—PIT, 2s. GALLERY, 1s.—Half price, a Quarter before NINE

W. BIRD, PRINTER, CARDIFF.

Programme of the Crockherbtown Theatre 1841.   *(Mr. & Mrs. B.J. Weston).*

investigate why the money ran out before everyone had been paid.

Despite its more bizarre features, many of the greatest names on the British stage trod the boards of the Theatre

Royal during its 50 year history. Mrs. Macready was the firs lessee of the theatre and, for 5 years, she persuaded a numbe of outstanding actors to visit Cardiff. In 1827 her stepson the great W.S. Macready, performed in his most famous role as *Macbeth*, to be followed soon afterwards by Sarah Siddons, another renowned Shakespearian actress of he time, and Edmund Keane whose reputation as a player of tragedy was unrivalled.

The Crockherbtown Theatre proudly proclaimed that i could cater for every taste, ranging from opera or Shakespeare to pantomime. From time to time the entertainment was provided by travelling "stock companies" under an actor-manager. This could result in a most strenuous life for the actors, who were not only expected to perform in several short plays during the evening, but also had to learn their parts in all of them. The advertisement issued by Mr. Braid in November 1841, is typical as he informs the public of an evening's entertainment that includes a comedy, a song and a three-act play. The show began at 7 p.m. and probably continued until 11 o'clock or even later.

The Theatre Royal came to a sudden and dramatic finale on the night of 11/12 December 1877. At 4 a.m. a passer-by noticed flames coming from the building. Possibly straw used in the previous evening's performance of *Scamps of London*, had caught fire and smouldered for several hours To make matters worse, the fire brigade was tending another fire in Canton and did not arrive on the scene until 40 minutes after the flames were first noticed. The reporter for the *South Wales Daily News*, wrote, "the blaze of the conflagration was a striking sight, illuminating the whole neighbourhood, and making a lurid glare on the sky". The fire was extinguished by 8.30 a.m. but by that time the building was a smouldering shell.

For a few years the site lay derelict. Then James Howell owner of the famous store in Cardiff, formed a consortium to build an hotel on the site. Apart from the theatre, Bradley's house also passed into oblivion and in their place arose the Park Hotel. James Howell provided half of the consortium's investment and he ensured that he would get some return on this considerable outlay by insisting that buyers and

Park Hotel soon after its opening 1895. *(Cardiff Central Library)*.

commercial travellers, who wished to do business with him, must stay at the Park Hotel. It is a splendid example of Victorian Gothic architecture, one of the most attractive buildings in Cardiff, though its graceful facade has been unkindly labelled "a watered down version of the Louvre".

James Howell was never a man for half measures and, when the new hotel opened its doors in April 1885, the interior reflected the fertile imagination of its major shareholder. One hundred bedrooms were available for weary travellers while their entertainment and comfort were provided in the hotel's smoke rooms, banqueting halls, coffee rooms and billiard halls. Along the length of the Queen Street facade was a row of shops and the hotel even had its own pub, the Park Vaults, as popular today as it was a hundred years ago.

Another feature of the enterprise was a magnificent concert hall which could seat 2,500 people. The Park Hall opened it doors on 28 April 1885 with a rendering of Handel's *Messiah*, performed by the Cardiff Choral Society. Many famous orators were to speak in this fine building, among them Winston Churchill who was invited by the Cardiff Naturalists' Society in 1900 to tell of his exciting adventures in South Africa. Later the Park Hall became a popular cinema, a role that it fulfilled until its closure in

1971. Today the once packed auditorium is the hotel car park and the foyer serves as a conference room.

Less than a year after the fire in Crockherbtown, a New Theatre Royal was opened in Wood Street. It had a superb stage but the view of the audience was somewhat restricted. The theatre, later known as the "Prince of Wales" and now an amusement arcade, had many setbacks ranging from fire to bankruptcy but it continued to give live performances until 1957. Today the principal playhouse in Cardiff is the New Theatre, just a short distance from the Park Hotel where actors often stay on the site where Macready, Keen and Sarah Siddons once captivated their audiences.

PARK HALL, CARDIFF.

The Committee of the Cardiff Naturalists Society beg to announce that Mr.

Winston Churchill, M.P.

Will give his deeply interesting Lecture, entitled :

"THE WAR AS I SAW IT"

ON

THURSDAY EVENING, NOVEMBER 29th, 1900, at 8.

The Lecture will be illustrated by Lantern Slides from Photos.

Mr. J. J. NEALE (*President of the Cardiff Naturalists Society*), will preside.

Doors open at 7.30.   Lecture at 8.   Carriages at 9.45.

RESERVED SEATS Balcony, Front Row, 7 6; Other Seats in Balcony, 5 : Area, 3 6; UNRESERVED SEATS, 2 .

Winston Churchill at the Park Hall 1900.   *(Cardiff Naturalists Society)*

58

THE FIRST CHIEF CONSTABLE

In the tower of St. John's Church, at first floor level, a tablet stands as a memorial to Jeremiah Box Stockdale, the first superintendent of police in Cardiff. For 34 years, at a time when Cardiff was being transformed from a small town into a great but sometimes violent and turbulent seaport, Stockdale was responsible for the safety of its citizens.

In 1835, for the first time, the borough council was elected by the ratepayers of Cardiff. An early problem for the newly formed corporation was the question of protecting its citizens. In a small town, where everyone was on familiar terms with his neighbour, watchmen and parish constables had assumed responsibility for public safety since the Middle Ages but now the population of Cardiff had reached 6,000 and was rising rapidly. Presumably impressed by the success of Sir Robert Peel in forming the Metropolitan Police a few years earlier, the Watch Committee decided to recruit "a London policeman" to organise the local constabulary.

Plaque to the memory of Jeremiah Box Stockdale.   *(Ian Morgan).*

Their choice was Jeremiah Stockdale. Though he was only 30 years old, his life had already been eventful. While little more than a teenager, he had caught the eye of Viscountess Kirkwall, a pillar of London society. She persuaded him to enlist as a lieutenant in a mercenary army which was sailing to Spain to fight for Queen Donna Maria. The Viscountess presented Stockdale with a handsomely bound pocket book and several pages of kindly advice written in her own hand. This was about all Jeremiah ever received for his endeavours. He was invalided home from Spain, apparently without receiving any pay, and on the return journey his ship ran into a severe gale during which all the passengers' luggage was jettisoned overboard. On landing at Portsmouth, possessing nothing more than the clothes he was wearing, Jeremiah set off for London to join the Metropolitan Police.

When he came to Cardiff in 1836, the new Superintendent of Police was an impressive figure. Over six feet tall, he was said to be "as straight as a lamp post and as stiff as an iron bar". He had a liking for elaborate uniforms and cut a fine figure with his dark blue tunic, his trousers trimmed with red cord, a peaked cap, and a sword belt that was presumably a relic of his military career. The former County Gaol in

Jeremiah Box
Stockdale.
*(South Wales
Police Museum).*

60

St. Mary Street was given to Stockdale as a police station and the old Town Hall served as a lock-up.

A far from generous budget made a daunting task even more difficult. Jeremiah was forced to supplement his own salary by acting as mine host at the Cardiff Boat public house in Womanby Street. Not surprisingly, in view of his limited resources, Stockdale's earliest recruits did not inspire public confidence. All three of his constables were nearing the geriatric stage, while his fourth pillar of support, Sergeant Aubrey, had the dubious distinction of never arresting anyone. He preferred to dispense his own justice at the scene of the crime. The policemen were equipped with an oil lamp at night, a truncheon, a pair of handcuffs and a rattle, presumably to summon reinforcements. An irate councillor described Stockdale's recruits as "a ragged regiment" but really it was a case of getting what you pay for and that was very little indeed. Complaints about the police were frequent and in 1850 every meeting of the Watch Committee dealt with an average of 3 misdemeanours, the most common of which were drunkenness on duty, assault, the frequenting of brothels and incivility.

Apart from building up the local constabulary, Stockdale had to patrol the streets, act as a detective and also take responsibility for the fire brigade. His own personality and physical strength were often enough to command respect and, within days of his appointment, he reported a disturbance in Womanby Street where a crowd was watching a fight but, as he informed the magistrate, "my appearance separated them".

With such a tiny force at his disposal, Jeremiah was always prepared to lead from the front. In 1840 a number of sea captains had been assaulted and robbed at night near the newly built West Dock. Stockdale, dressed as a sailor complete with sou'wester, set himself up as bait. Soon, aware that 3 men were stalking him, he broke into a run and was pursued along the side of the dock. One of the rogues, unluckily for him as it proved, outpaced the other two and caught up with the police chief who turned and floored him with a right hook. The other two men ran off but the dazed mugger was arrested and later transported for 7 years.

Stockdale's most famous arrest followed the Chartist Rising of 1839. After the battle between the Chartists and the military outside the Westgate Hotel in Newport, both the militia and Stockdale's tiny police force were put on full alert just in case the agitation spread to Cardiff. As it proved, the uprising was soon crushed and there were no disturbances in Cardiff, but one of the ringleaders, Zephaniah Williams, sought sanctuary in the town. He went into hiding at the Sea Lock Hotel, alongside the Glamorganshire Canal, and from there he boarded a ship that would take him to France. Unfortunately for Williams, his notoriety led to his discovery before the ship could sail. Stockdale and a constable rowed out to the vessel and put handcuffs on Williams before he was fully awake. There was a reward of £100 for his capture but, as this did not apply to police officers, Stockdale never collected a penny. Williams, in common with the other Chartist leaders, was sentenced to death but this was later commuted to transportation for life.

Undoubtedly, Stockdale lived in violent times. The first recorded race riot in Cardiff occurred in 1848 after a Welshman, Thomas Lewis, was fatally stabbed by an Irish immigrant. His name was John Connors and a lynch mob,

Old Sea Lock Hotel 1891.   *(Cardiff Central Library).*

seeking to impose its own justice, rampaged through the district of Newtown, searching for him. He was eventually arrested at Pontypridd and convicted of manslaughter. In due course he was transported to Botany Bay but, at Lewis's funeral, Irish navvies armed themselves with pick-axes along the route, just in case there was a further outbreak of violence.

As Cardiff became one of the world's great seaports, Tiger Bay began to gain its notorious reputation as a den of vice and iniquity. Opium dens, posing as Chinese laundries, started to make an appearance in Butetown. Sailors found themselves shanghaied and relieved of their worldly wealth after an encounter with the ladies of the night. Prostitution was so commonplace that one policeman claimed to have raided more than 80 brothels during a single year.

There were bound to be occasions when the limited means at Stockdale's disposal could not prevent bloodshed. In 1856, during a fight between Greek and American seamen, both sides resorted to knives and revolvers but these were "encounters of such frequent occurrence that little notice was taken of them". However, during the Crimean War, he was able to defuse a potentially dangerous situation, when Turkish and Russian ships were moored alongside each other in the East Dock. Upon being informed that the Turks were sharpening their scimitars and making threatening gestures towards the Russian crew, Stockdale ordered the vessels to be berthed on opposite sides of the dock. Once the Russian ship had departed, he found an excuse to detain the Turks for another 3 days.

The growing borough of Cardiff needed an organised fire service and this too became Stockdale's responsibility. In 1840 there were 2 manual fire engines under the old Town Hall in High Street. These could be dragged to a blaze which was then fought with water drawn from wells, or the river, or the Glamorganshire Canal. By the time Stockdale left office a fire engine house, entered from Guildhall Place, had been constructed at the rear of the new Town Hall. Fire hydrants were placed at convenient points and the borough could boast a horse drawn steam fire engine. Two regular firemen from the police supervised 12 civilian volunteers

The Cardiff Police Fire Brigade 1874.   *(Cardiff Central Library).*

who responded to an emergency either from their homes or their places of work.

Sadly, Jeremiah passed his last year in office under a cloud. The premises of one of the Watch Committee, Mr. Whiffen, were burgled in Church Street and, when the committee next met, Whiffen launched into a tirade, claiming that the police force was "not in such a good condition as it might be". A sub-committee reached the conclusion that Stockdale had outlived his usefulness and ought to resign. Following an appeal, when Jeremiah had to plead with the Corporation not to "terminate the connection which has so long subsisted between them and an old and tried servant, under the circumstances so opposed to his wishes and so painful to his feelings", the decision was reversed, though only by 1 vote. This seems to be an appalling example of ingratitude when we realise that, after the inauspicious beginnings of the Cardiff police, Stockdale had built up an efficient force of 60 men that included a police band to entertain the public in Sophia Gardens.

After Stockdale's death in 1870, the more grateful citizens of Cardiff showed their appreciation of his work by erecting 2 monuments in his memory. One of these was a fountain which stood for many years in Adamsdown Square but has

Stockdale Memorial Fountain in Adamsdown Square 1939.   *(H.B. Priestley).*

now disappeared. However, the tablet in St. John's Church was erected by public subscription and is a lasting tribute to the man who, with only the minimum of resources, established an effective, modern police force in Cardiff.

Memorial Plaque to John Bird.   *(Ian Morgan).*

High Corner House 1877.   *(Cardiff Central Library).*

THE DIARIES OF JOHN BIRD

A tablet, once in the Aldermen's aisle but now in the tower of St. John's Church, was donated by the second Marquis of Bute, "as a token of affectionate respect" to the memory of John Bird. It was a fitting tribute to the man who had served the Bute family faithfully for nearly 50 years. Bird himself had prospered from this relationship and, when he died in 1840, he was an alderman, a magistrate and one of the wealthiest men in Cardiff. However, more interesting than the offices Bird held, are the diaries he kept which cover the period from 1790-1802 and the year 1826. The entries make fascinating reading not only of Bird's relationship with the Butes, but also of the changes that were taking place in Cardiff at this time and the issues that confronted its citizens.

Even before John was born at the castle in 1761, his family had served the lords of Cardiff Castle for more than half a century. His own career was linked to the interests of the first Marquis of Bute and by 1790 he was clerk to the Bute estate and lived in the High Corner House at the entrance to the castle. To a large extent, Bird's diaries are reminders of information he ought to pass on to the Marquis or his agent, Henry Hollier. Such reminders were essential as it was never an easy matter to communicate with either of them.

Through his marriage to Charlotte Windsor in 1766, the first Marquis controlled 11,000 acres of land in Cardiff and Glamorgan but, though he once wrote, "that without being excessively attentive, accurate and watchful, an estate must suffer", he never applied this principle to himself. He rarely visited Cardiff and showed little concern for its community. In 1815 a surveyor commented, "I never saw an estate in a more neglected condition" and for this Henry Hollier must share the blame.

Apart from acting as the agent for the Bute estate, Hollier also held the posts of Town Clerk for Cardiff, Collector of HM Customs and Receiver-general of taxes for Glamorgan.

First Marquis of Bute.   *(Cardiff Castle Collection*

He was also a rogue who took full advantage of his statu
to enrich himself, with the result that his administration c
the estate was deplorable. In fact, he swindled both th
Crown and his employer, eventually being prosecuted by th
former and dismissed by the latter. His dubious practices
and the failure of the Marquis to detect them, placed a majc
responsibility on Bird who worked ceaselessly in hi
master's service.

His diaries are full of matters relating to the Bute famil
and its interests. Many of his entries are concerned with suc
mundane matters as collection of rents and arrears of ren
book-keeping and accounts, but sometimes he is caught u
in more turbulent events. In June 1799 he accompanied th
Deputy Sheriff and the Town Clerk on an expedition to expe

quatters from the Heath, where they had illegally built huts nd cottages. The squatters did not take kindly to eviction nd in particular their "Amazonian women", as Bird calls hem, offered stiff resistance with pitchforks and similar mplements. Bird rode back to Town to fetch the cavalry who urnt down the cot where the fighting was fiercest. His day vas far from over as the battle continued and he was lispatched to Caerphilly for reinforcements. They were not equired as the squatters had already accepted defeat but, for ome time afterwards, Bird had to suffer jibes about his kirmish with the "Amazonian women".

Though Bird did his best to ensure that Bute was fully nformed about what was happening in Cardiff and 3lamorgan, the Marquis rarely showed much interest or ppreciation for his efforts. Indeed he is very alarmed in 801 when Colonel Capper tells him, "Lord Bute asks for 'e Bird. He says that he hears from ye sometimes", with the mphasis on the last word. Bird wonders: should he be more ommunicative?

Should he submit a weekly journal? Has he been discreet nough? He goes on to say that he would, "rejoice at having line of conduct marked out", but no guidance was

The Bute Mausoleum at St. Margaret's Church.   *(Diane Walker/John Morgan).*

Portrait of John Bird.

John Bird.

(Cardiff Central Library

orthcoming. Bird also received short shrift when he delicately asked for an increase in his £40 a year salary after pressure of work on the Bute estate had forced him to give up his coaching business.

The first Marquis was a selfish, inconsiderate spendthrift whose principal talent lay in the art of marrying well. After Charlotte's death in 1800, Bute persuaded Fanny Coutts, the daughter of the wealthy banker, to marry him. Her wedding gift to him was a dowry of £100,000. When he died in 1814, few in South Wales mourned him and it is rather ironic that he is the only one of the Marquises of Bute to be buried in Cardiff. He was laid to rest in a special mausoleum which had been built some years earlier to house the remains of his first wife and their son, John. The mausoleum, at St. Margaret's Church in Roath, has since been re-designed and within it members of the Bute family are interred in seven plain polished tombs, fashioned from red granite and similar to those which contain the remains of the czars of Russia in St. Petersburg.

John Bird's diary paints a vivid word picture of the Cardiff he knew, with his comments on Parliamentary elections, the visits of the judges and conditions at the County Gaol. He reflects on the state of the roads and the problems of travelling by coach. He gives eye-witness accounts of the rebuilding of Cardiff Bridge and the construction of the Glamorganshire Canal. An understandable pride emerges when Bird describes how he purchased Cardiff's first printing press at a cost of 17 guineas in 1791, an achievement that allowed him to produce the earliest trade directory for the town a few years later. Particularly interesting are his observations of the town during the Napoleonic wars.

After the abortive French assault on Fishguard in February 1797, Judge George Hardinge complimented those who had repelled the enemy, "convinced that the spirit of the ancient Britons would be ever alive to resist the common enemy and to ward off the impending blow". Bird indicates a flurry of activity as the Cardiff Volunteers expanded their numbers and began exercising on the Castle Green. It is almost possible to conjure up visions of Dad's Army as Colonel Capper indicates his readiness to teach the men in "the use of the Great Guns, should any be sent down". No everyone was a happy volunteer. In 1793 Bird relates how 45 sailors, armed with cutlasses and bludgeons, marched through Cardiff, hotly pursued by the press gang. A Rumney, an ugly confrontation was watched by interested spectators who eventually intervened to save the outnumbered press gang from the wrath of the sailors. The gang "very prudently declined the attack and the Towns people treated the Sailors with a pint of ale each".

Judge Hardinge is also aware of the danger of civil disobedience as the spectre of famine stalked the land. By 1800 the price of corn was rocketing and John Bird assisted Colonel Capper in the distribution of a shipment of grain raised by public subscription. Fears of revolution, anti royalist agitation and "internal commotions" are voiced but though the gentry of Glamorgan urge the Marquis to take the initiative in organising relief for the poor, their plea falls on deaf ears.

The diary for 1826, by which time Bird was semi-retired is more detailed on social matters. He was now enjoying a happy relationship with the second Marquis of Bute who

Cardiff Castle from the West 1820. *(Cardiff Central Library)*

could never be accused of neglecting his duties or his estate. Unlike his grandfather, the Marquis recognised Bird's contribution in building up that estate, granting him a pension of £150 a year and taking the trouble to call on him when he is suffering from rheumatism. Bird still spends a great deal of his time at the castle, sometimes on business but often for pleasure. In June a ball, attended by 400 people, was probably a celebration of Lord James Stuart's election victory a few days earlier. All appeared "highly delighted" as dancing continued until 5 a.m. Bird clearly enjoys hobnobbing with important people and during 1826 he not only dined with the Butes and the judges on their visits to Cardiff but also met the Duke of Gloucester, the first royal visitor to Cardiff since Charles I. During February of that year, John spent a few days in London, where he was presented to the Duke of Sussex and revelled in "a most delightful evening" at the Freemasons' Tavern. There was a price to pay as Bird records "a very rough night" during the 27 hour return journey by stage-coach to Cardiff.

The obituaries for John Bird in 1840 tell of "a gentleman of much local influence, a kind-hearted, intelligent and useful member of the community". At times he appears rather pompous but there is always a genuine decency in the man and a strong sense of duty. He may have enriched himself by hitching his star to that of the Butes but they were fortunate to have such a loyal servant. Bird was a cultured man who loved good music and played a major part in establishing Cardiff's first theatre. We are fortunate that his diaries give us an intriguing glimpse of the changes that were taking place in Cardiff during his lifetime.

A PROTESTANT MARTYR

In James Howell's store in St. Mary Street, a plaque tells u
that, "Near this spot suffered for the truth ... Rawlins White
a fisherman of this town". Who was this fisherman? How and
why had he suffered? In searching for the answers to these
questions we must return to the sixteenth century, when the
state demanded religious conformity from everyone and
failure to accept this fact of life was to invite persecution and
martyrdom. Three Protestants, none of whom was Welsh
were to die for their faith in Wales and one of these was
Rawlins White.

He was a native of Somerset who came to live in Cardiff
about 1535 and made his home near the Town Quay. He
rented 5 henges or weirs along the River Taff and for many
years seems to have lived a quiet life. All this was to change
as a result of the Reformation when Rawlins was already

Memorial to Rawlins White in Howell's Store.   *(Ian Morgan)*

74

approaching his sixtieth birthday. He became an ardent Protestant or, as he would put it, "a diligent hearer and seeker-out of the truth". Unable to read himself, White sent his son to school and every night, year in and year out, the boy read to his father from the Bible. Blessed with a wonderful memory, capable of absorbing and quoting lengthy passages of scripture, Rawlins prepared himself to preach among the people of Cardiff and the Vale of Glamorgan, denouncing the Roman Catholic Church and all that it represented.

For 5 years he attracted little attention but his faith was put to the test when Queen Mary came to the throne in 1553. She was determined to restore the authority of the Roman Catholic Church and anyone who opposed that policy could expect short shrift. New religious laws were introduced which were intended to silence the Protestant point of view but White had no intention of meekly complying with any restrictions on his freedom of speech. He deliberately flouted the law and continued to preach in his own fiery

The former Bishop's Palace at Mathern. *(Dennis Morgan).*

manner until he attracted the attention of Anthony Kitchin, the Bishop of Llandaff, whose duty it was to uphold the command of the sovereign in matters of religion. At first Kitchin tried to ignore him but White "looked every hour to go to prison". His arrest was inevitable and he was incarcerated first at Chepstow and then at Cardiff Castle. At this stage, White could have escaped without difficulty and probably the Bishop would have been relieved if he had done so. Certainly, it is fair to assume that Kitchin, who was always content to serve Protestant and Catholic monarchs alike so long as he remained Bishop of Llandaff, found the attitude of this stubborn old man incomprehensible.

However, there is little doubt that Rawlins had his eye on the martyr's crown and, when he was brought to trial at the Bishop's palace in Mathern, not far from Chepstow, he rejected any thoughts of compromise. The drama of the occasion had attracted a great gathering and, when Kitchin accused him of being "obstinate and wilful", White turned to the onlookers with the plea, "If there be one brother amongst you, the same one bear witness at the day of judgement that I bow not to this idol". Sentence of death was passed upon him and he was transferred to the gaol in High Street under the Town Hall, "a very dark, loathsome and most vile prison". His biographer tells us that he spent the last 3 weeks of his life praying and singing psalms, "which godly exercises he always used both at Cardiff Castle and at all other places".

On Market Day, 30 March 1555, the old man, now in his seventieth year, was brought to his place of execution near the market place in High Street. He was wearing what he described as his "wedding garments": a long shirt, an old russet coat and a pair of leather buskin boots. When he saw the armed guard sent to escort him from the prison he cried out "What meaneth all this? I will not run away". Like all martyrs, Rawlins White would die bravely, though once he burst into tears when he saw his wife and children, "weeping and making great lamentation", among the large crowd. The moment of uncertainty passed as he confessed to his great friend, John Dane, "I am sorely tempted. If I weaken again, hold your finger up and I shall remember myself". Then, as

Woodcut depicting the Martyrdom of Rawlins White. *(Cardiff Central Library)*.

the blacksmith began to chain him to the stake, Rawlins urged him to make the chain fast, "for it may be that the flesh would strive mightily".

The funeral pyre of wood, straw and reeds were laid around him and White assisted his executioners in this grisly task, "with such a cheerful countenance that all present were astonished". A Roman Catholic priest addressed the large crowd, warning them that this was the fate of all heretics, but White, determined as ever to have the last word, denounced him as "a false prophet and a naughty hypocrite". As the straw was lit, the fire crackled and smoked before erupting into a great flame. Even while his body was being devoured in the fire, Rawlins White cried out, "O Lord, receive my soul". His biographer said that in death, "he seemed to shed his three score and ten years and his head and beard appeared altogether angelical".

Memorial to Rawlins White in St. John's Church.   *(Ian Morgan).*

His martyrdom was not forgotten. John Dane carefully noted the details of his life and death and, 20 years later, the story of the Cardiff fisherman was recorded for posterity in Bishop Foxe's *Book of Martyrs*. Much later, in the eighteenth century, a small, weather-beaten plaque seems to have been fixed to the Town Hall in High Street but any trace of this monument disappeared when the building was pulled down in 1861. However, there is a modern memorial in St. John's Church where the head of Rawlins White is one of a number carved in stone on the shafts upholding the roof of the chancel.

The bronze tablet in Howell's store was originally provided by 2 anonymous donors and was unveiled in Bethany Chapel by the Lord Mayor of Cardiff, W.S. Crossman, in 1907. The chapel was sold to Howell's Store in 1964 and its front has been incorporated into the men's department. On this facade, as you enter the store from St. Mary Street, you can see the plaque bearing testimony to the execution of Rawlins White. A fanatic he may have been but his tale is one of courage, faith and stubborn determination. These reasons are good enough to honour his memory.

Howell's Store 1995. *(Ian Morgan).*

THE FATHER OF MODERN CARDIFF

The statue of the second Marquis of Bute, known locally as "The Monument", shows him dressed as a Roman senator. Originally the statue was erected outside the Town Hall in High Street but, after a number of complaints that it was obstructing the traffic, the decision was taken to re-site it at the southern end of St. Mary Street.

John Crichton Stuart entered into a rich inheritance after the death of his grandfather in 1814. He owned the land on which most of the old borough of Cardiff was situated and held the rights over its foreshore and waterfront. Perhaps most important of all, his legacy included extensive estates in Glamorgan under which lay those rich seams of Welsh coal soon to be in demand from every corner of the world. The Marquis took full advantage of his riches, adding to them whenever he could, thus strengthening his social, economic and political standing in South Wales. Yet he was also a man of vision who regarded the proper use of his wealth to be almost a sacred trust and it was this sense of duty that led him to become the most important influence in the development of nineteenth century Cardiff.

He had a reputation for being dour, arrogant and ruthless, the same qualities that were to be found in his friend, the Duke of Wellington. He suffered from an eye disease which was so serious that he found difficulty in reading and replying to any correspondence. It also made him so accident-prone that any form of exercise, such as riding or even walking, was fraught with personal danger. Even so, his physical handicaps did not prevent him from being industrious and conscientious to a degree that was almost an obsession. It seems bizarre that the owner of such vast estates should be concerned about the broken flagpole at Cardiff Castle, or whether the castle dog was properly tied up at night, but the Marquis expected to be informed about everything, however trivial, that touched upon his affairs.

Statue of the Second Marquis of Bute.   *(Ian Morgan).*

St. John's Church in the Mid-nineteenth Century. *(Cardiff Central Library)*.

Bute could only spare the time to visit his Welsh estates for a few weeks each year in spring and autumn but his reception at Cardiff was almost like a royal progress. When the Marquis came to worship at St. John's Church, "the captain of the militia towed his lordship along Church Street as every man doffed his hat and every woman bobbed". His agent, Edward Priest Richards, prepared for the visit well in advance. Which were the deserving causes the Marquis ought to patronise? Who should be offered leases for the mineral rights on the Bute estates? Which tradesmen ought to be favoured with new contracts? Who deserved one of those eagerly sought invitations to the banquet at the castle?

This kind of influence was only possible while Cardiff remained a small borough but the Marquis regarded the exercising of such patronage as his right. He expected the town council to carry out his wishes and regarded the parliamentary constituency as his personal gift. This attitude even applied to his brother, Lord James, who was MP for Cardiff. When the two men disagreed over the question of parliamentary reform in the 1831 election, Bute ensured that his brother was defeated by giving his backing to a candidate opposed to reform. In this same election, in his role as Lord Lieutenant, the Marquis instructed the members of the Glamorgan militia to vote for his nominee and those who did not, were accused of mutiny.

Bute may have been a reactionary Tory on that issue but there is ample evidence that he was warmly regarded by the humbler members of society. On more than one occasion, he showed his antagonism towards the ironmasters of Merthyr because of the manner in which they used their power to exploit the poor. He objected to the lack of safety regulations in their mines, the private prisons that some of the ironmasters retained for disobedient employees and, most of all, the truck system whereby wages were partly paid in tokens valid only at the company shop.

The Marquis was the patron of numerous charitable causes such as the Cardiff Infirmary and contributed to many of them generously. He was particularly interested in education and provided sites and endowments for 17 schools in Glamorgan, among them the St. John's church school in Crockherbtown. Bute's reputation among the poor was also enhanced by personal acts of kindness: £10 a year "to Mrs. Roderick for the maintenance of her idiot son"; £1 a month "to the post boy who broke his leg" delivering letters to the castle; £5 to Edward Williams' wife "to enable her to have the benefit of sea bathing at Swansea". Yet the Marquis had

St. John's Church School 1912.   *(Cardiff Central Library).*

little patience with the idle poor and showed scant sympathy towards the Irish immigrants who arrived in Cardiff "with pestilence on their backs and famine in their stomachs".

So far as Cardiff was concerned, the building of the first Bute Dock was the most important decision the Marquis ever made. At first he was reluctant to make such a huge capital investment but his agent persuaded him that the dock would pay for itself once it began to export mineral wealth from the Welsh coalfield. When the West Dock was opened on 8 October 1839, it was the first to be built in South Wales and that evening, at a dinner to celebrate the event, the American Consul forecast that the dock would bring prosperity to Cardiff, "as long as grass grew and water flowed".

He was right. The building of the West Dock gave Cardiff an advantage over the other ports of South Wales just as the Welsh coalfield was about to reveal its treasures to the world. The dock soon became overcrowded and too small for the phenomenal growth of the Welsh coal industry, and other docks were built as the nineteenth century ran its course. The population of Cardiff multiplied at an astonishing rate as a small town was transformed into a great city.

Bute West Dock about 1900. *(Fred Jones).*

The Marquis made this considerable investment more from a sense of duty than for personal gain. His initial misgivings proved to be well founded and he was forever scrutinising the accounts as the cost of the dock soared. It is ironic that the Cardiff docks never made a profit for the Butes, though the family prospered greatly from the royalties on their mineral wealth.

The Marquis was also troubled with personal problems. His first wife, Lady North, brought him land and money in her dowry, but when she died in 1841 she had borne him no children. Four years later he was married again, this time to Lady Sophia Hastings, but at the age of 52 the likelihood of fathering a son to continue his work must have appeared remote. The prospect of leaving the Bute estates to his brother, Lord James, with whom he had quarrelled over the Reform Bill, could not have been attractive to him. So we can imagine his great joy when Lady Sophia bore him a son and heir in September 1847.

He was to know the boy only a short time. On 18 March 1848 Bute was attending a banquet at Cardiff Castle, when suddenly he felt unwell and retired to his dressing room. Soon afterwards he was found dead, apparently from a heart attack. The funeral procession on a wet, dismal morning was over a mile and a half long, as the Marquis was carried along St. Mary Street and Bute Road to the dock he had opened 9 years earlier. All parts of the community in Cardiff and Glamorgan were represented to bid him farewell, as the coffin was taken by sea to Bristol and then to its final resting place at Kirtling in Cambridgeshire.

"Weep, sons of Cambria, weep at the loss of such a benefactor", wrote T.E. Clarke in the *Merthyr Guardian*. Perhaps he was being too deferential to the man who had founded his newspaper. Nevertheless, it is true to say that the second Marquis of Bute paved the way for Cardiff to become a thriving seaport and eventually a great city. Thus he deserves the accolade, by which he is remembered, as "The father of modern Cardiff".

The Second Marquis of Bute.   *(Cardiff Castle Collection).*

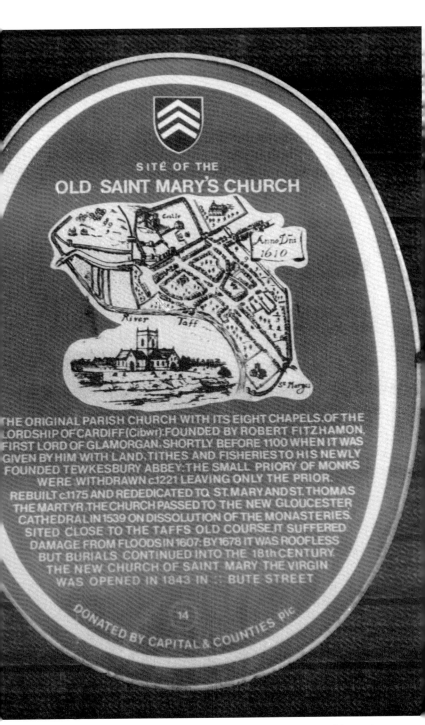

SITE OF THE

OLD SAINT MARY'S CHURCH

THE ORIGINAL PARISH CHURCH WITH ITS EIGHT CHAPELS, OF THE LORDSHIP OF CARDIFF (Cibwr) FOUNDED BY ROBERT FITZ HAMON, FIRST LORD OF GLAMORGAN, SHORTLY BEFORE 1100 WHEN IT WAS GIVEN BY HIM WITH LAND, TITHES AND FISHERIES TO HIS NEWLY FOUNDED TEWKESBURY ABBEY: THE SMALL PRIORY OF MONKS WERE WITHDRAWN c.1221 LEAVING ONLY THE PRIOR. REBUILT c.1175 AND REDEDICATED TO ST. MARY AND ST. THOMAS THE MARTYR, THE CHURCH PASSED TO THE NEW GLOUCESTER CATHEDRAL IN 1539 ON DISSOLUTION OF THE MONASTERIES. SITED CLOSE TO THE TAFFS OLD COURSE, IT SUFFERED DAMAGE FROM FLOODS IN 1607: BY 1678 IT WAS ROOFLESS BUT BURIALS CONTINUED INTO THE 18th CENTURY. THE NEW CHURCH OF SAINT MARY THE VIRGIN WAS OPENED IN 1843 IN BUTE STREET

14

DONATED BY CAPITAL & COUNTIES PLC

Plaque of St. Mary's Church, Great Western Lane.   *(Ian Morgan).*

ST MARY'S CHURCH

Nowadays, the church of St. Mary the Virgin is to be found in Bute Road but the earliest church to bear that name occupied a site at the southern end of St. Mary Street. It was sited near the Prince of Wales Theatre and, on the wall at the back of the theatre, we can see the outline of a church marked in white stone, perhaps a recognition of the original use of this site. The blue plaque, erected in memory of St. Mary's Church, can be seen on the wall of the car park opposite.

When the Normans conquered Morgannwg at the end of the eleventh century, Robert Fitzhamon, the first lord of Glamorgan, decided that Cardiff should be his principal borough in the region. To meet the spiritual needs of the settlement which grew up around the castle, Fitzhamon decided to endow a monastic church that would be administered by a prior and monks from Tewkesbury Abbey.

In 1100, St. Mary's Church was built a few hundred yards to the south of the castle on open land near the river, which

Outline of the Church at the rear of the Prince of Wales Theatre 1995. *(Ian Morgan).*

was not, as future events were to prove, a particularly well chosen location. We cannot speculate on the appearance of this first church because within a hundred years it was being rebuilt. There is no description of this building either but John Speed's map of Cardiff in 1610 indicates a Norman church in the shape of a cross. Its dominant feature is its lofty central tower. In earlier times there would have been monastic buildings but these had disappeared by the seventeenth century. The monks of St. Mary's were recalled to Tewkesbury as early as 1221 and, before the end of the fourteenth century, the prior was also withdrawn. Henceforth, the parish was served by a vicar, assisted by his chaplains.

However, despite these changes, St. Mary's remained firmly under the control of Tewkesbury Abbey until the Reformation, reaping the benefit of the tithes and rents collected on its behalf in Cardiff. These were quite considerable as the church collected its tithes at a barn in Wharton Street and owned several properties in St. Mary Street and Crockerton. The vicarage itself stood in the centre of High Street, near the Town Hall. Known locally as the Middle Pinion, it was a gift from an unknown donor on condition that a light was kept burning in the church to his memory. There were also many outlying chapels in and around Cardiff that were administered from St. Mary's. The most important of these was St. John's Church but St. Mary's also had jurisdiction over places of worship as far afield as Roath, Llanishen and Lisvane. The revenues from all these chapels contributed to the upkeep of their mother church or were donated to Tewkesbury Abbey. Yet, even in the Middle Ages, the chapel of St. John soon became more popular, more wealthy and attracted a larger congregation than St. Mary's. After the Reformation, all the dependent chapels were to become parishes in their own right and the Rectory of St. Mary's was granted to the Dean and Chapter of Gloucester.

Soon the church fell into a state of terminal decline. The root of its problems lay with its ill-chosen site of low lying land, where flooding was frequent and holding the waters of the Taff at bay was a costly business. In the Middle Ages,

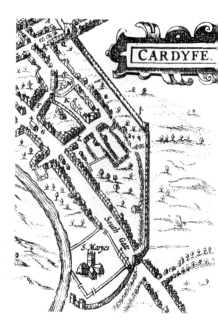

St. Mary's Church
as it appeared on
Speed's Map 1610.
*(Cardiff Central
Library).*

some of the money needed for this purpose was obtained
from people who feared the terrors of purgatory and eternal
damnation. They often left a legacy to the church so that a
chaplain could say mass for their souls. These chantries, as
they were called, were abolished in the sweeping changes
that occurred during the Reformation and, with money no
longer available for repairs, the defences against the
incursions of the river began to disintegrate. In 1578 the
whole parish was seriously flooded and before the end of the
century the boundary wall of the churchyard was beginning
to collapse.

During the Great Flood of 1607, which wreaked such
destruction in and around Cardiff, St. Mary's felt the full
force of the elements as a contemporary chronicler wrote
that, "a great part of the church ... was beaten down with the
water". From this document arose a myth that the flood spelt
the end for the mother church of Cardiff but Speed's map 3
years later shows that it was still more or less intact.
However, Speed observed that the Taff was "a foe of St.
Mary's Church ... undermining her foundations and
threatening her fall". Certainly the invasion from the sea had
permanently swept away a corner of the churchyard and

brought nearer the day when St. Mary's would be abandoned by its flock.

The building never really recovered from this disaster though services were held in the church until the middle of the seventeenth century. The townspeople of Cardiff preferred to spend whatever funds were available on St. John's Church which stood on safer, higher ground.

Even the clergy appeared to lose interest in St. Mary's and, during the Civil War, the Roundheads removed its vicar, Theodore Price, for neglecting his office. The complaint seems to be justified as one parishioner claimed that no sermon had been preached in the church for 14 years. The Civil War hastened the decline of St. Mary's, when damage was caused to the fabric during the two Royalist assaults on Cardiff Castle. By 1678 the central tower had collapsed through the roof and the church was no more than an empty shell.

No services were held in the church after the Restoration of Charles II, though burials in the churchyard continued until 1707 and children were baptised in the ruins as late as the 1730's. Gradually, as the remaining stones of St. Mary's were taken for other building work, all traces of the old church disappeared from human view. Yet, at the beginning of the nineteenth century, a portion of the ancient burial ground still remained and was enclosed with a wall but sometimes there were macabre reminders of the past. A letter to the *South Wales Daily News* in 1907 recalled that 60 years earlier "there were frequently to be seen portions of human skeleton exposed when a heavy flood washed off some of the river bank of St. Mary Street".

The parishioners of St. Mary's retained their own gallery in St. John's which now became the centre of spiritual life in Cardiff until the first Bute Dock was opened in 1839. As the population of Butetown began to expand, the second Marquis of Bute encouraged the idea of rebuilding St. Mary's Church in Bute Road. After purchasing the living from Gloucester Cathedral, he provided a site and £1,000 towards the building costs. Fund raising took many forms, including a poem by the Poet Laureate, William Wordsworth.

St. Mary's Church
in Bute Road 1995.
(Ian Morgan).

"When Severn's sweeping flow had overthrown
St. Mary's Church, the preacher then would cry,
Thus Christian people, God his might hath shown,
That ye to him your love may testify;
Haste, and rebuild the pile."

The new church, built in a Gothic style, is one of the best examples of early Victorian architecture in Cardiff and is well worth a visit. When it was opened in December 1843 the bells rang out from St. John's, flags and banners gave a blaze of colour to Bute Street and St. Mary Street, while the ships in the dock raised their colours to salute the resurrection of the Church of St. Mary.

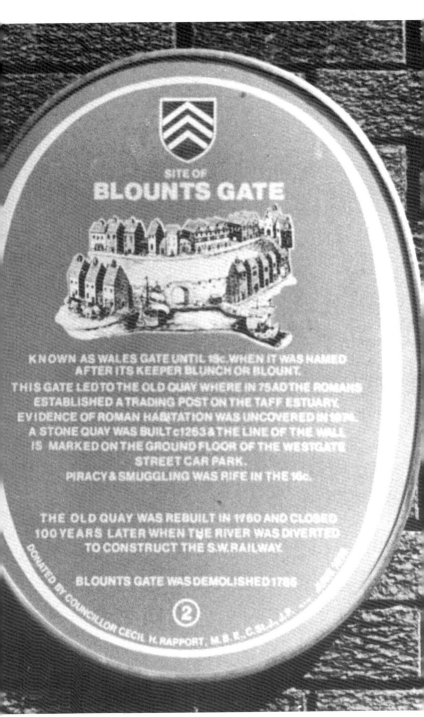

SITE OF
BLOUNTS GATE

KNOWN AS WALES GATE UNTIL 18c. WHEN IT WAS NAMED
AFTER ITS KEEPER BLUNCH OR BLOUNT.
THIS GATE LED TO THE OLD QUAY WHERE IN 75AD THE ROMANS
ESTABLISHED A TRADING POST ON THE TAFF ESTUARY.
EVIDENCE OF ROMAN HABITATION WAS UNCOVERED IN 1974.
A STONE QUAY WAS BUILT c1263 & THE LINE OF THE WALL
IS MARKED ON THE GROUND FLOOR OF THE WESTGATE
STREET CAR PARK.
PIRACY & SMUGGLING WAS RIFE IN THE 16c.

THE OLD QUAY WAS REBUILT IN 1760 AND CLOSED
100 YEARS LATER WHEN THE RIVER WAS DIVERTED
TO CONSTRUCT THE S.W. RAILWAY.

BLOUNTS GATE WAS DEMOLISHED 1785

②

DONATED BY COUNCILLOR CECIL H. RAPPORT, M.B.E., C.St.J. J.P.

Plaque of the Town Quay. *(Ian Morgan).*

THE TOWN QUAY AND THE GOLATE

A blue plaque, fixed to the wall of a car park at the junction of Westgate Street and Quay Street, indicates that the gateway to the Town Quay was situated near here. This knowledge comes as a surprise to many people since the nearest water is more than 200 metres away on the other side of the Cardiff Arms Park. Yet, until 150 years ago, the Taff flowed along what is now Westgate Street and, until the end of the eighteenth century, the quay was Cardiff's principal outlet to the sea.

In 1974, excavations revealed that the Romans used this site as a trading post. Later, the Danes were very active in the Bristol Channel and, while it is customary to portray the Norsemen as bloodthirsty warriors, they were also traders and merchants. While there is no archaeological evidence of a Viking presence in Cardiff, Womanby Street is a name of Scandinavian origin and it is possible that the Danes sailed their longboats up the Taff and established a base in this vicinity.

Quay Street 1995.

(Ian Morgan).

Originally, the quay was a wooden structure that was rebuilt in stone at some time during the thirteenth century. For the next 600 years, small vessels of 50 tons or so made a tortuous passage along the muddy estuary of the Taff to weigh anchor at the foot of Quay Street. In the Middle Ages, the Lord of Glamorgan collected the harbour dues from traders using the port and it was in his interests to ensure that it was properly maintained. Later, when Cardiff became a royal borough, the people of the town paid the cost of repairing the quay and dredging the mud banks. As the Taff was frequently in flood, erosion was a constant problem and a report of 1552 mentions that the Quay had been repaired three times in 20 years.

Blount's Gate, named after one of the mediaeval gatekeepers, stood at the entrance to the quay. The gate itself was not demolished until 1785 but the destructive force of the river had eaten away the town walls along its bank many years before, and their demise was further hastened by the ferocious onslaught of Owain Glyndwr in 1404.

In the sixteenth century, 10 merchant ships were trading from Cardiff. A few of them sailed as far as the Channel Islands and France but most were content to make a short

Cardiff from the South 1776 by Paul Sandby. *(Cardiff Central Library).*

journey to West Country ports such as Bridgwater Minehead and, most important of all, the "Welsh Back" in Bristol. Farmers used the quay regularly as they could obtain a better price for their butter, cheese, eggs and poultry on the other side of the Bristol Channel. People too found that it was more convenient to travel by sea, rather than along roads built a thousand years earlier by the Romans, and now filled with pot-holes.

A little further south of Quay Street another blue plaque commemorating The Golate, is attached to the wall of Golate House. This narrow lane leads from St. Mary Street to Westgate Street and, according to local legend, is so named because late arrivals, who had missed the boat at the quay, rushed down this alley-way to board their ship before it began its voyage down river. The story seems most unlikely and it is much more probable that the word is derived from the "Gulleygate" that provided access to the river at this point.

The Golate 1995.   *(Dennis Morgan)*

GOLATE

KNOWN VARIOUSLY AS PORTH LLONGAU SHIPS GATE, FROG LANE, GOLYGATE, GULLEYGATE, LOCAL TRADITION LINKS THE NAME WITH THOSE DAYS WHEN LATE ARRIVALS CAUGHT THE OUTWARD BOUND SHIPS FROM FURTHER UP RIVER. PIRACY WAS RIFE IN THE 16c & CARDIFF GREW RICH ON THEIR TRAFFIC.

1576 JOHN CALLICE OF CARDIFF BROUGHT IN A SPANISH GALLEON — THE BOOTY SOLD TO GENTRY AND CITIZENS. ARMS SMUGGLING TO SPAIN WAS NOT UNKNOWN IN 16c & BARBARY PIRATES RAIDING THE COASTS, CAPTURING CARDIFF SHIPS, BRINGING POVERTY TO THE TOWN IN THE 17c.

BACONS SOLIDS THE CONTRACT GUNS OF ANTHONY BACON OF CYFARTHFA WERE SHIPPED TO AMERICA DURING THE 1775-83 WAR OF INDEPENDENCE FROM CANNON WHARF BELOW GOLATE

③

DONATED BY RAVENSEFT PROPERTIES LTD. JANUARY 1976

Plaque of The Golate. *(Ian Morgan).*

While the plaque informs us that guns, stamped with the inscription, "Bacon's solids", were shipped from Cannon Wharf in the American War of Independence, there is no mention of the gun-running 200 years earlier which brought rich pickings to the Mathew family of Llandaff. Cannon of excellent quality were manufactured at Radyr but Edmund Mathew found he could obtain a better price by exporting them to Spain, a nation that was busily preparing an armada for the invasion of the British Isles. Despite the efforts of the Privy Council to prevent this illegal trade, Mathew is estimated to have exported more than 150 tons of weapons from Cardiff quite openly between 1582 and 1600, because "the port officers were poor and dared not displease him".

Both plaques relate how the Bristol Channel once offered the prospect of easy pickings for pirates. In the early fifteenth century, Colyn Dolphyn, a villain from Brittany, established a base for himself on Lundy island and preyed on unwary vessels setting out from the ports of South Wales. Even the gentry were not safe and one of his victims was Sir Henry Stradling, the wealthy owner of St. Donat's Castle. He was apprehended while crossing from Somerset to Glamorgan and was only released when his family paid a ransom of £1,400.

The most notorious acts of piracy, involving the borough of Cardiff, occurred in the reign of Queen Elizabeth when the port became a favourite haunt of John Callice. Throughout South Wales, this rogue had reliable spies who passed on information when an unarmed vessel, with a profitable cargo on board, was about to sail. After ambushing his victim at sea, Callice looked for a safe haven where he could dispose of the booty without attracting the unwelcome attentions of the law. Usually he sailed into a sheltered harbour at Penarth or Sully, where he unloaded his ship before using Cardiff as a market for his ill-gotten gains.

In 1574 he captured a Breton fishing boat and sold its contents in Cardiff and Bristol. Two years afterwards he captured a Spanish vessel with its consignment of wool bound for Bruges and once again he found a ready market in Cardiff. The townspeople were happy enough to purchase salt, fish or a few bottles of wine at bargain prices but it proved to be embarrassing, especially for merchants, when their town was known everywhere as, "a general resort of pirates".

Obviously, Callice could only act in this high-handed manner with the connivance of the leading citizens of Cardiff who also happened to control the forces of law and order. When the victims of piracy protested, the Admiralty Court in London sent its representative to Cardiff with orders to restore all stolen property but he was treated with contempt, both by the pirates and by their accomplices. Such brazen arrogance compelled the Privy Council to appoint a special commission. In due course it reported that the local magistrates, including the Sheriff of Glamorgan, were not only aiding and abetting the pirates but were also indulging in riotous behaviour with them at "taverns and tippling houses in Penarth and Cardiff".

Eventually, after the ringleaders were fined and warned about their future behaviour, Callice decided it was time to depart for new horizons. Soon afterwards he was captured off the Isle of Wight but still managed to gain a pardon. He turned Queen's evidence against one of his colleagues, who was captured and hanged, thus proving there is no honour among thieves.

In the seventeenth century piracy was finally suppressed and the Town Quay was able to resume its normal service, but by 1800 the volume of trade at Cardiff lagged far behind that of Swansea, Llanelli and the Pembrokeshire ports. The cost of maintaining the quay became increasingly expensive, as sediment built up in the Taff and at times the river was little more than a succession of slimy mud banks. Larger vessels could not enter the harbour at all and smaller craft could only negotiate the mud flats at high tide. Special water bailiffs were appointed to levy charges for repairing the quay which continued to be used until 1840. The first stage in its decline coincided with the opening of the Glamorganshire Canal and the quay came to the end of its useful life when the West Dock was completed in 1839.

Throughout the centuries, flooding had been a cause of considerable destruction in Cardiff. In 1848 the Town Council saw a golden opportunity to deal with this problem, when Isambard Kingdom Brunel visited Cardiff to plan the route of the South Wales Railway. By hacking out a new cut 200 metres to the west, Brunel and his navvies altered the course of the Taff to its modern route. Some years were to pass before the old river bed was filled in but eventually Westgate Street and the Cardiff Arms Park were built on the land reclaimed from the river.

When the photograph of Quay Street was taken in 1891, most of the buildings were private dwelling houses, or tradesmen's workshops and offices. The building in the foreground on the right has the appearance of a stable but it was from here that the Cardiff and South Wales Hide, Skin and Fat Market ran its business. It may seem unhygienic to handle the remains of slaughtered animals when people are living nearby but the Victorians were unconcerned about such niceties. The public house in the photograph bears the nautical name of "The Ship on the Launch" and a tavern may have existed on this site when John Callice's spies were prowling Quay Street 300 years earlier. While the ground floor of this building has changed considerably, the two

Quay Street 1891. *(Cardiff Central Library).*

upper storeys are recognisable as part of the present Model Inn.

The fascination of Quay Street and The Golate lies in the past and today they are no more than byways, offering a short cut for the crowds surging towards the National Stadium on the day of a big match. Yet, though the buildings are modern, the narrow roadways still follow the same course as in those distant days when lawless villains mingled with busy merchants, sailors and townsfolk hurrying towards Cardiff's gateway to the sea.

A RURITANIAN KING

At 95 Cowbridge Road East, opposite St. David's Hospital, a blue plaque bears the inscription,

> *This boy became a Ruritanian King*
> *Who gave his people dreams and songs to sing.*

The "Ruritanian King", born at this house on 15 January 1893, was Ivor Novello Davies, one of the greatest names the British Theatre has ever produced. His father, David Davies, was head of the Cardiff Rates Office. He was a cautious individual who never saw his son's music as more than a hobby, but Ivor's mother, Clara Novello Davies, had very different ambitions for the boy on whom she doted. Already a celebrity in her own right and intensely proud of her Welsh heritage, she was not only a well-known music teacher, but her Welsh Ladies' Choir was as famous in the Victorian age as the Vienna Boys' Choir is today.

Certain that she had given birth to a genius, Madam Clara, as she was known, ensured that her son was steeped in a

Number
95 Cowbridge Road
East, 1995.
(Ian Morgan).

102

musical environment almost from birth. She had hopes that he would become a composer of operas and, as a child prodigy, he performed with some of the great opera singers of the day. The house in Cowbridge Road was known as "the Grove of the Nightingale" and, when he was only seven years old, Ivor was taught to sing *Abide with me* by Dame Clara Butt. A year later he was capable of singing a duet with Adelina Patti.

Even at that tender age, Ivor was already fascinated by the stage. Clara tried to discourage him from any thoughts of a theatrical career, urging him instead to concentrate on his music. So, from her point of view, it was a mistake to buy Ivor a toy theatre, for which he wrote plays, invented his own characters, and then charged his friends to watch the final production.

Ivor possessed a beautiful voice that was to win him a place at the famous Magdalen College School in Oxford. He was the leading light in its famous choir but, when his voice broke, his parents were unable to afford the expense of a university education. His ever-prudent father suggested a comfortable job in a Cardiff shipping office but this idea was strenuously opposed both by Ivor and his mother. Clara had now moved her studio to 11 Cathedral Road and, for the next

Cowbridge Road 1910.   *(Cardiff Central Library).*

103

few years, her "darling boy" assisted her at concerts, taught music and began composing it. Today, this house contains an interesting collection of items and photographs from Ivor's career.

His first composition was accepted by the famous Boosey company when he was 17 and about this time Ivor and his mother took up residence in London at a flat above the Strand theatre in Aldwych. For the next few years he wrote song after song, most of which were returned to him with a polite rejection.

Then the First World War began and Clara urged Ivor to compose a song for the troops far away from home. At first he showed little enthusiasm but, when Clara threatened to submit a jingoistic work of her own, *Keep the Flag A'flying*, Ivor thought it was such an appalling song that he agreed to provide an alternative. An American lady, Lena Ford, who had written some lyrics for his earlier music, offered to assist him with the words. One day, as they were deliberating and looking out of the window at a blackening, stormy sky, the maid entered the room to put logs on the fire. Ivor exclaimed. "That is what I want. Something to remind the boys of home by the fireside" So the first 2 lines of an immortal song emerged;

Madam Clara and Ivor.   *(Cardiff Central Library)*

"Keep the home fires burning,
While your hearts are yearning."

Lena Ford completed the lyrics and soon afterwards *Keep the Home Fires Burning* was sung for the first time at a Sunday concert in the Alhambra theatre. Accompanied by the band of the Grenadier Guards, the audience sang the chorus half a dozen times. Next day the music shops were inundated with requests for the sheet music and Ivor went on to acquire the considerable sum of £15,000 for the masterpiece he had reluctantly written.

During the First World War, Ivor served in the Royal Naval Air Service and also contributed to concert parties for the troops. He wrote several numbers for wartime shows and, after the war, showed his versatility by launching a successful film career. He became one of the most popular film stars of the 1920's, both in Britain and in the United States where, at one point, he was earning £350 a week.

But his first love always lay with the theatre and he turned his back on Hollywood fame to take part in *The Rat*, a stage thriller he had written himself. It ran for 283 performances in the West End and was later adapted for the cinema. Indeed, 2 sequels followed and Ivor starred in both of them. So successful were his films that, by the end of the 1920's, he was seriously thinking of concentrating on a film career since, apart from *The Rat*, his efforts on the stage had met with little success.

All this was to change in the 1930's when Novello found his true vocation and began to produce the greatest musicals of the day. The first of these spectaculars was launched almost by accident. One day in 1934 Ivor lunched with H.M. Tennent, the managing director of the Theatre Royal in Drury Lane. The theatre had recently suffered a number of box office disasters and Tennent was desperate for a successful show. Ivor virtually worked out a plot over lunch for a Ruritanian musical which included an assassination attempt, a rebellion, a spectacular shipwreck and even included a place in the climax for the new invention of television. Tennent, caught up in this burst of enthusiasm, agreed to stage the production and Ivor went away to write

Ivor Novello.
(Stewart Williams).

and plan the first of his great musicals. He called it *Glamorous Night* and for 7 months in 1935 the show played to packed houses. Even King George V and Queen Mary came to see it.

Glamorous Night was followed by a succession of other great musicals, including *Careless Rapture, Crest of the Wave* and *The Dancing Years*. These shows not only made Novello a rich man but offered escapism from the ever darkening world of the 1930's. Ivor was not unaware of the storm clouds gathering in Europe and, while *The Dancing Years* is a romance, there are grim undertones as the hero is a Jewish actor whose career and liberty are threatened by the Nazis.

The Novello musicals were to play on throughout the Blitz of the Second World War but the conflict brought personal disaster to the man who had given joy to so many people. Never a particularly worldly person, Ivor was prepared to tolerate the blackout, the Blitz and wartime restrictions but the great pride and joy of his life was his Rolls-Royce. Petrol of course was rationed but an enthusiastic admirer assured him that he could transfer the car to her firm and use it at weekends. Unfortunately, the lady in question had no authority to make such an offer and

Plaque to the memory of Ivor Novello.   *(Ian Morgan).*

Ivor was arrested for contravening the wartime regulations on the use of motor cars. He was sentenced to a month's imprisonment in Wormwood Scrubs. To such a sensitive man it was a devastating experience and it was of little comfort to know that an old admirer, Winston Churchill, felt he had been harshly treated. When he had served his sentence, he wondered what kind of reception his public would give him. He need not have worried. On the night he returned to play in *The Dancing Years*, the end of the show was greeted with thunderous applause.

Until the end of his life, Ivor continued to produce musical masterpieces. *Perchance to Dream* opened at the Hippodrome in April 1945 and the show ran for more than 2 years. Its great hit song, *We'll Gather Lilacs*, was to become almost as famous as *Keep the Home Fires Burning*.

Ivor considered *King's Rhapsody*, the last of his musicals, to be his finest work and, as it turned out, it was also to provide his final curtain. After the evening performance on 5 March 1951, Ivor complained of pains in his arms and chest. It was a coronary thrombosis and early next morning, at the age of 58, Ivor died. For his funeral in London, the streets were packed as if for a royal farewell. A bouquet of white lilacs adorned the coffin and, to the strain of *We'll gather Lilacs*, Ivor was laid to rest at Golders Green Crematorium.

The Ruritanian romances of Ivor Novello are no longer fashionable but his songs live on and are often played at concerts today. Ivor's reputation was made in the West End Theatre, especially Drury Lane, and he rarely returned to Cardiff after he became famous. Even so, plans are now advanced to erect a statue in Cardiff Bay to honour the genius of a man whose music, which gave pleasure to millions of people, was nurtured in his native city.

Grave of E.T. Willows. *(Ian Morgan).*

A PIONEER OF FLYING

Ernest Thompson Willows, whose grave is to be found in Cathays Cemetery, was killed in a tragic air accident on 3 August 1926. He was piloting balloon flights at a flower show in Hoo Park, near Bedford, and had already made several ascents when disaster struck. While the balloon was being winched back to the ground, a sudden gust of wind caught the trail rope and it became entangled in a tree. As the basket broke away from the balloon, Willows and his four passengers fell 100 feet to their deaths.

Ernest Willows was born at 11 Newport Road, now a part of Cardiff University, in July 1886. Some years later the family moved to 2 Dumfries Place where his father had a dental practice. Ernest too began to follow his father's career but soon became much more excited in the prospect of making and flying airships. He once said, "As a boy I remember jumping off a bank with an open umbrella in my hand, just to make believe I was flying". He was fortunate that he had a father who admired his son's initiative, was not

Willows' Airship over the City Hall 1910.   *(Cardiff Central Library)*.

averse to a gamble, and was prepared to finance him in the designing and building of his airships.

Though he had no formal training as an engineer, Willows experimented in a large shed on East Moors. The performance of early airships depended on the strength and direction of the wind but Willows designed a sausage-shaped craft that could be steered by a pilot using a motor and screw propellers. Such dirigibles were to be the predecessors of the Zeppelins in the First World War. On 5 September 1905 the first Willows' airship rose over the moors and was successfully manoeuvred 120 feet above the ground by its young pilot.

The year 1910 proved to be the most eventful in Willows' life. In an airship, twice the capacity of his earlier model, he collected a prize of £50 when he became the first man to fly over Cardiff. It was on 4 June that he navigated this craft from East Moors to the City Hall, landing near the statue of Lord Tredegar. Since it was only 7 o'clock in the morning, no more than a few hundred people were present but three days later a crowd of 40,000 saw him repeat the flight.

Willows celebrated his 24th birthday on 11 July with a flight from Cheltenham to Cardiff and other exciting

E.T. Willows.
*(Cardiff Central
Library)*.

adventures were soon to follow. On 6 August his airship was the first to cross the Bristol Channel as he set out for London. The intention was to land at the Crystal Palace but Willows ran out of petrol and the propellers could not be used. The craft drifted for a few miles when an astonished householder was woken up at 5.30 a.m. by the sound of a trail rope rattling on his roof, to be followed by a request, "Please haul me in". Some railwaymen on their way to work lent a hand and Willows was safely down. The following day, after refilling with petrol, he arrived at the Crystal Palace.

Congratulations were showered on him including one from the Cardiff City Council but, as so often in his life, nothing was forthcoming in terms of financial backing. Willows decided an international success was the only way to persuade backers to loosen their purse strings. Accordingly, he planned a non-stop flight from London to Paris in a new airship which he christened *City of Cardiff*.

On 4 November Willows and his mechanic, Frank Gooden, set forth from Wormwood Scrubs airfield on his greatest adventure. Despite thick belts of fog, they crossed the English Channel without mishap but then their luck changed. Gooden lost his maps and mechanical problems forced them to land near Douai, 100 miles from Paris. Repairs were completed by 15 November but it was several more weeks before the journey was completed. First the airship was damaged in a strong crosswind and then the propeller shaft suffered a fracture. Finally a rail strike held up repairs and it was not until 28 December that Willows saw the Eiffel Tower just as the sun was setting. Willows and Gooden must have felt the delays were worth while as a cheering French crowd carried them shoulder high from the airfield. The French press acclaimed their feat and Willows enjoyed a celebrity status as he spent the next week or so offering Parisians flights around their city at 200 francs a time.

He planned to fly on to the Pyrenees but French customs officials told him that he must leave the country or pay £30 import duty on the gas in his ship. Willows decided to come home, confident that his exploits would bring him commercial success. He was to be disappointed. An appeal in his native Cardiff barely raised £50 and he decided to move his business to the Midlands. In Birmingham he designed the Willows IV airship that was capable of carrying two passengers and attracted the interest of the War Office. Willows realised that it would be many years before dirigibles became a feasible form of transport and he was thinking in terms of a craft which, if war came, would be capable of naval scouting duties.

The Willows IV was inspected by Lieutenant Waterlow of the Royal Flying Corps and he reported, that while the airship was unsuitable from a military standpoint, it could be useful for training purposes. He concluded, "Given financial backing, Mr. Willows should be able to turn out a very fine ship". Alas, that financial backing was never forthcoming and at the end of 1912 Willows was declared bankrupt.

Once again his father, who never lost faith in his talented if unfortunate son, came to the rescue and in 1913 a new company was formed in Cardiff under the name of J.T. Willows. Apart from building airships, the company offered flying lessons and traded generally in the aeronautics business. His support was to bring Mr. Willows Snr. close to

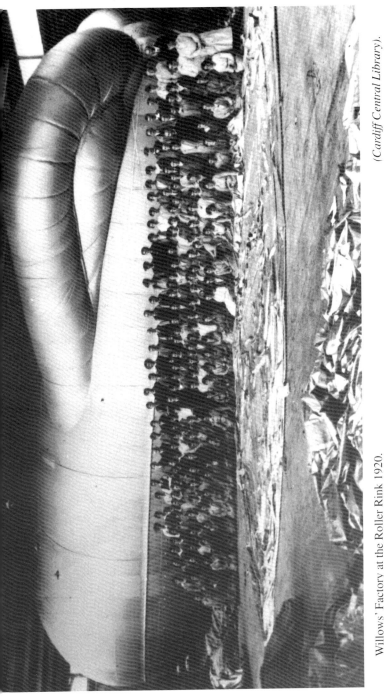

Willows' Factory at the Roller Rink 1920.

(Cardiff Central Library).

bankruptcy himself though he eventually succeeded in discharging himself from this humiliating position.

E.T. Willows still had contacts in the aviation world and, at the outbreak of the First World War, he was working for George Holt Thomas as the chief engineer of Airships Ltd., a company with its headquarters at Merton in London. The ideas Willows had been advocating for so long at last began to attract the interest of the Admiralty. Lord Fisher, the First Sea Lord, saw advantages in a fleet of small airships to guard the coast and search for submarines. The Admiralty wanted a dirigible that was easy to fly and could be assembled quickly and cheaply. The craft that Willows delivered to the Royal Naval Air Service in March 1915 was regarded as too complicated but the Blimps, subsequently developed by the Air Service, incorporated much of his thinking.

After accepting a commission in the Royal Flying Corps, Willows went on to serve his country in another capacity when he played an important role in the defence of London against German air raids. He designed a steel curtain which could be suspended by kite balloons of the type used in the Second World War. These curtains were hung over London at a height of 10,000 feet to protect the city against low-flying enemy aircraft. His efforts saved both life and property in the Metropolis and he was officially commended for his "valuable services" to the defence of London.

Yet Willows' contribution to the war effort brought him little tangible reward. Though they used many of his ideas, it was the Air Service that developed the Blimp and, while Willows submitted a claim of £30,000 for his work with kite balloons, the Treasury fought his claim and he eventually collected only £500. Willows returned to civilian life and, in the last few months of the War, manufactured kite balloons for the War Department at the former Roller Skating Rink in Westgate Street.

Even this source of income dried up when the Armistice was signed. The dreams and hopes Willows had once had for his beloved airships were finished and there is something almost pathetic about the last few years of his life. To support his family, he purchased a schooner for £3,500 but ill luck, never far away from him, struck once more. The *Imogen* went aground on a shingle bank near the Isle of

Wight and broke up. Once again Willows was penniless and his last contact with the world of flying lay in offering balloon rides for pleasure. The last of these was to kill him and the manner in which Willows died seems almost inevitable, for his whole life has an element of tragedy in it.

Willows School 1995.   *(Ian Morgan).*

Apart from his business failures he suffered personal anguish. Of his four children, one died in infancy from meningitis and another was to be killed in a motor-cycle accident in 1932.

Perhaps it was as well that this ill-starred airman never lived to witness the demise of the airship after a series of disasters in the 1930's. The future of flying lay with the fixed wing aircraft and, though he sometimes talked about building an aeroplane, Willows always placed his faith in the dirigible. While it is true that he was no businessman and often gave the impression his inventions should sell themselves, he had a creative mind that could have benefited the nation with better government support. It is rather sad that this pioneer of flight is largely forgotten in his native Cardiff, even though a school and a road bear his name, not far from the moors where he first began his experiments in flight.

INDEX